THE COLOSSUS OF ROADS

Myth and Symbol along the American Highway

THE COLOSSUS OF ROADS

Myth and Symbol along the American Highway

Karal Ann Marling

with an album of
Minnesota photographs by Liz Harrison
and additional photography by Bruce White

UNIVERSITY OF MINNESOTA PRESS • MINNEAPOLIS

FRONTISPIECE
Great Sphinx Hole at Goofy Golf,
Panama City, Florida. Photograph
©JOHN MARGOLIES/ESTO, 1979.

Copyright ©1984 by the University of Minnesota
All rights reserved.
Published by the University of Minnesota Press,
2037 University Avenue Southeast, Minneapolis MN 55414
Printed in the United States of America

Library of Congress Cataloging in Publication Data

Marling, Karal Ann.
  The colossus of roads.

  Includes bibliographical references.
  1. Folk art – United States – Psychological aspects.
  2. United States – Popular culture – Psychological aspects.
  3. Symbolism in art – United States. 4. Folklore – United
  States – Themes, motives. I. Title.
  NK805.M27   1984   745'.0973   84-5079
  ISBN 0-8166-1302-8
  ISBN 0-8166-1303-6 (pbk.)

The University of Minnesota
is an equal-opportunity
educator and employer.

For my brother, Gregory

Auto City USA is as near as the city line: a bazaar, auto style, where the Ford dealers' flags fly, the symbolic Hawaiian Pineapple vies with the Coach and Horses for your rest stop, the eclectic Swiss Chalet with the Monticello Motel for your night stop and the auto graveyard cowers guiltily behind its beautification of six street trees beside the Victorian Gothic manor left over from an earlier era, now a wholesale plumbing supplier. Signs and wires deck the wider landscape, caging your head in a virile mobil which screams "GAS" and "EAT" and whispers "Fifth Street" and "US66."

Denise Scott Brown and Robert Venturi
The Highway
1970

Stop. Ahead. Five hundred yards. See. Camera bugs welcome. Fur Seal Caves. Rocks of Mystery. Frontier Village. Jungle Land. Reptile Farm (see them milk the diamond-backs). Indian Burial Mounds. Alligator Gardens. Swamp Creatures. Big Game Country. Little Africa. Bibletown. Old West Museum. Wild Animal Ranch (see rare white deer). . . . Stop. The tourists stop, happy for an excuse to pull off the dangerous hot highways; a place for mommie and the kids to pee, a place to stretch the legs, reload the Kodak, mail postcards, buy cigarettes, drink a Coke, see. See. See something they've never seen before. Gila monster. King cobra. Billy the Kid's shootin' iron. . . . Humpty Dumpty in papier mache. Or, in the case of the Capt. Kendrick Memorial Hot Dog Wildlife Preserve, a flea circus and the meaning of meaning.

It is a hot dog stand. . . . A glorified hot dog stand. . . . A giant hot dog is beached like a whale on the rooftop. It is made of painted wood and is surrounded by an entourage of painted figures in a painted landscape; by comets and peaks. The big sausage is the first thing one sees. It is visible for a mile around.

Tom Robbins
Another Roadside Attraction
1971

Contents

Preface

It is high summer on the prairie. A Saturday afternoon. Getting on toward 2:30 or 3:00, maybe. According to the time-temperature clock blinking over a deserted Main Street in western Minnesota, the mercury stands at 103°. The lights that show the time are burned out. The temperature flashes, though. Those big, red numbers even *look* hot. The numbers shimmer in the still air but nothing else moves, except our rent-a-car. Inside, with the air conditioner cranked up to "maximum cool," the heat still bastes the skin and sears the eyelids.

Bob's driving. He's been driving around Minnesota for almost a month now, in the heat and the ferocious hot-weather thunderstorms, wondering why he didn't spend the summer in the library. There must be easier ways for a graduate student to make a buck. Today, the heat's getting to him. During our last stop—and a rare fit of self-pity—he wrote "Chauffeur" beneath his name in the guest book at the Chamber of Commerce tourist office.

I'm riding shotgun, ignoring Bob's testy mood, reading the map. The map needs reading; we're seldom on the superhighway. And I'm past feeling Minnesota's extremes of climate, too cold in the winter, way too hot in the summer. 103° doesn't bother me much. What does is the oppressive flatness of all the back roads and the Main Streets. We drove through the Valley of the Jolly Green Giant, near Le Sueur, a couple of weeks ago, and I still remember the rise of the ground and the swoop of the road. The puniest hills are major events in our long, hot summer.

But hills are few and far between. Instead, there are hours of straight roads, lined by endless, even fields of beans and corn, or stands of timber merging with the mirror surfaces of shallow lakes scooped from the level surface of the ground. The sky is too big out here, a nagging weight on the back of the neck, a burden borne on protesting shoulders. The sky tires a person out. The land is too flat, loudly proclaiming its bigness and its blustering expansiveness and its crude power by that insistent, uninterrupted sprawl.

Pascal was only half right, I think. The terror of infinite spaces increases in the eerie silence of a hot Saturday afternoon but the space itself is the frightening thing, when it comes in the huge, flat segments that are the highway and Main Street and then the highway again, zooming from horizon to horizon, ironed smooth by the distant, unreachable shimmer of a mirage gliding before the turning wheels, over the hot asphalt.

The prospect of the blazing road beyond the drowsy blink of the time-temperature clock is not enticing. When it's hot, I am too often mesmerized into daydreams by the gleam of the long, flat vista ahead. The map slips to the floor, all unnoticed. Once, we missed a turn that way, and Bob, furious, slammed into a feed and grain co-op to ask directions. What he almost blurted out, he told me later, was the kind of question that arises only when the academic overdoses on real life: "Which way to the American Dream?"

Students lie sometimes to please their teachers. (In fact, poor Bob would sooner die than invite the ridicule of strangers with arcane queries about the American Dream!) Yet this transparent fib did please, and tease at the edges of sensibility. It hinted at something we both felt keenly enough, although neither of us, before that sweltering afternoon at the head of Main Street, could have put a name to a muddle of vague, troublesome yearnings stirred by the road on its flight through the distinctive landscape of the midwestern plains. The Dream was no lie after all! Infinity seemed so close—just down the road. Why, you could almost see the edge of the world, up there ahead, where the highway met the sky!

So close. So attainable. And because it always seems so very near, that far horizon beckons us forward, tempting us to chase the illusion that is, perhaps, our dreams. The goal, at any rate, is something wondrous, something seen clearly only in the mind's eye, something that lies just beyond the limits of mundane vision, something that will always elude the most ardent pursuers, as it hastens backward, into the future.

The beckoning vision propels us restlessly down the highway. The roadside cornfields, the shallow lakes that skim past the windows, are all of a piece; the flatness, the sameness, and the steady, unwinding cadence of the real-life present make it easy to look away, to pass by and to hurry onward. But what is out there, down the road, way up ahead—the future—retains its pull by virtue of its roseate unreality. Fantasies and dreams are lovelier than a thousand dusty fields: the forms and phantasms that glimmer at the end of the road spring not from the soil of western Minnesota but from the fertile reaches of the imagination. The inferno of the highway presents a paradox. Monotony promises enchantment. Bored and bedazzled, we rush headlong down the weary miles.

But wait a minute. Stop. What's that? Off to the right up there, across from the supermarket, just before the highway resumes its race toward the sunset. Stop! It's a monstrous fish—a 15-foot-long fantasy in cement, beached on a plot of grass by the edge of Main Street. The chicken-wire armature shows through in a couple of spots and the sticky green paint is bleached out and blistered by the sun. The leprous mouth gapes, revealing sickly pink innards, two cigarette butts, and a crumpled Pepsi can. And there it lies, in all its scabby, goofy glory, flanked by a pair of benches and a picnic table, in the scrap of grassy park that faces the local lake—the sort of site once favored for solemn war memorials, with cannon, and cannon balls, and verdigris veterans.

The fish is far too big for the tiny lake, one of Minnesota's fabled 10,000, to be sure, but a tepid pond by most objective standards. The crowd in attendance is also too big for the lake, on the shoreline of which clusters, it seems, the entire local population, sweating profusely and studiously ignoring the fish. The older folks sit quietly in the picnic pavilion, out of the sun. Moms and Dads lie prone along the waterline, like the unburied dead, too hot to move, scarcely breathing. Even the kids are silent and sluggish: they slump in the shallow water, up to their necks, and whine a little, from time to time, very softly.

Only the tourists stir. We circle the fish, chattering, poking and prodding as we go, looking for photogenic angles. A drunk lolling on the park bench closest to the tail looks up, and belches, and buries his face in his hands again. And, suddenly energized, we trot back up Main Street toward the Rexall at a fair clip, past the motionless drunk and all the sun-stunned bathers, in search of souvenirs—some memento to prove that this was not a dream, some artifact to reify another odd little episode in a summer punctuated with odd little hitches in the steady flow of time and highway and the flat roadside landscape.

The blast of frigid air that whooshes into the street when the door is opened forms a ghostly vapor trail above the sidewalk; inside, the drugstore is as cold and as silent as the grave and empty, except for one lone clerk, standing motionless behind the counter. We twirl the postcard rack, and wince at its protesting squeaks, deafening in the palpable hush. No concrete fishes here. A brace of beady-eyed pheasants and a hunter with a hound, separated by a kind of scroll where the name of the town is supposed to be printed: this one says nothing at all. Two views of a highway, also divided by a blank banner meant for imprinting. On the top, a road zooming through flat, green pastures. On the bottom, the same road running past ranks of green, leafy trees. But no green concrete fish with lime-colored spots and fins.

No postcard of the fish. No evidence that Main Street put the fish out along the roadside for some reason and was prepared to admit some civic pride in ownership. Was it really ever there, this afternoon, on the sweltering shore of the lake, where nobody but the tourists paid it the slightest attention? Or are there far stranger sights along Main Street, more noteworthy curiosities beside which the big fish pales in local eyes? I want to rush back into the street, to verify a memory not ten minutes old, to scan the curbs, to check that the car's still there, ready to flee for the far horizon.

"Do you have picture-postcards with the fish on 'em?" Bob asks, cocking his thumb toward the street. "Oh, sure. Back here. How many do you want? No. They're free. You're welcome. You're not from around here. The Cities, huh? Hot, isn't it. Have a nice day." It's a very plain postcard. No fancy photography or crinkly edges or day-glo script. No blank spaces for imprints, either. Just the big green fish, seen in profile, centered on a swatch of green grass.

There is no middle distance in the picture—just the foreground, filled up by the big green fish, and a far-off, diminished background with two spindly green trees, a pair of spindly telephone poles, and

Main Street, the Rexall shriveled and flattened against the horizon line. Objects on the horizon seem small and low and mean. The big fish lying close to the camera's eye looms all the larger because it parodies the thrust of the horizon, mocking the magnetism of dreams that wait down the road, far away, where the sky begins or ends. The fish fills the field of vision, and blocks the beckoning vista. It fills the foreground of reality, asserting the claims of the tangible present over the call of the chimerical future.

In real life and in postcard view, the fish is too cumbersome, too awkwardly solid, too bulky to be ignored. The motorist can't glide by. Like a boulder on the highway, the material amplitude of the big fish stops traffic. A rooted mass at odds with the flight of the road, it vivifies a sense of place. We write out postcards for friends back home: "Wish you were here!" "Here" is strange and odd, the domain of lurid, monster fauna—dream turned to nightmare, the magical someday become a sweltering now, fantasy become a dense, disconcerting, impenetrable reality.

That torrid afternoon in western Minnesota is not unique; American reality is often larger than everyday life on sleepy weekends has any right to be. Tom Wolfe remarks upon "the Hog-stomping Baroque exuberance of American civilization." He probably hasn't seen the big green fish on Main Street, but time and again he has observed a certain native propensity for fiddling with scale. Scale is a judgment on the ordinary and the everyday: the Grand Canyon, the Astrodome (A wonder of the modern world, folks! Twice as large as the Colosseum of Old Rome!), the Gateway Arch, the Sears Tower, and the big green fish make tourists stop because they are anomalies, bigger—clearly bigger—than such things ought to be, disruptive features in the natural and the built environments. Seen against the measure of pokey little Main Streets skittering past the shores of placid lakes, they startle by their florid rhetoric, their grandiose aspirations. They brag and boast and holler and stomp, in a wild American orgy of self-assertion and desire.

So the pilgrims come, in pursuit of their dreams, steering by the giant arches and the towers, by the marvels of nature run wild, by the serried wonders and the big green fishes that are America's special landmarks on the highway between yesterday and tomorrow. Back home goes the message, scrawled on the backside of a huge, cement fish: "Wish you were here!" "Here" is a point, circled in red on the roadmap between the sureties of personal history and the giddy possibilities of what is yet to come, between home and the horizon. It is a place from which the tedious normality of daily life is missing. It is a place made for pioneers and pilgrims and tourists, a place for the dramatic arrivals and flamboyant departures that give to the weary transient the assurance of having come to someplace new. The miles and hours *have* indeed flown by. We *haven't* passed that big green fish before! Roadside monuments mark off the frontiers and boundaries of "here." By increments of "heres," we feel our way ever onward. "Which way to the American Dream?" Why, it's up the road, there. You'll come to a big green concrete fish off to your right and then. . . .

The essay that follows is about our travels through Minnesota last summer, in fitful pursuit of the American Dream. It is about the aesthetic of the Midwest, about midwestern stories and symbols. It is also about time and place in America, and history, and nostalgia, and the frontier. It is about an American penchant for commemorating our lost frontiers with gigantic statuary—anonymous, vernacular sculpture for the most part, or, less often, the work of well-known artists momentarily bent on popular appeal. It is about the distinctive feel and the cultural texture of the 1920s and 30s in America's heartland, and what remains of that anxious, questing spirit in the roadside colossi still made and solemnly dedicated and chuckled over by Minnesotans and their neighbors—by midwesterners—today. It is about anxiety and humor and tourism. It is about going places. It is about high summer on the prairie, just last year, and about the winter of 1937, when it was bitterly cold on the shores of Lake Bemidji, up north in Minnesota. . . .

TALL TALES, TRADEMARKS, AND THE GREAT GATSBY
Midwestern Space Defined

The winter of 1937 was bitterly cold in north-west Minnesota. A furious Arctic wind drove the temperature to 30° below, and there it stayed. Between the worst weather on record and the economic chill of the Great Depression, tourism had all but ceased. Huddled together around the stove in the back room of a Bemidji store, the regulars fretted over a business climate as frigid as the gale howling outdoors. They consoled themselves with familiar, local stories, calibrated to the grotesque extremes registered on the plummeting thermometer.

"Ever hear about Paul Bunyan and the Year of the Two Winters?" Sure. That was the winter so cold the snow turned blue, the very color of Paul's pet ox. Why, it stayed so cold for so long, the mercury took three whole years to creep back up to zero. Yes, sir! Old Paul's loggers, they tried to keep their faces warm by growing beards for the season, but the winter dragged on into summer, and then into fall, and those beards grew to incredible lengths. "Some of the boys had the ends of 'em knitted into sox!" chirped the bright-eyed old-timer closest to the stove rail.[1]

In the 1930s, it seemed, everybody knew Bemidji's mythical tales of the stupendous logging boss named Paul Bunyan. Novelist John Dos Passos appropriated the legend to symbolize the American worker, grown larger-than-life in the strength of collective action, and thus feared by "the Chamber of Commerce" and the business establishment. His *Nineteen Nineteen*, published in 1932, described Wesley Everest, the martyred sawmill organizer from the state of Washington, as "a logger like Paul Bunyan."

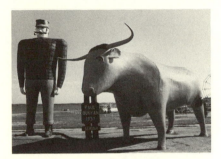

Paul Bunyan and Babe, the Blue Ox, built on the shore of Lake Bemidji, Minnesota, in 1937. Photo courtesy of State of Minnesota, Department of Economic Development.

Paul and Babe, as depicted in a promotional booklet for the Red River Lumber Company of Minneapolis in the 1920s. From an illustration by W. B. Laughead.

[T]he I.W.W. put the idea of industrial democracy in Paul Bunyan's head; wobbly organizers said the forests ought to belong to the whole people, said Paul Bunyan ought to be paid in real money instead of in company scrip. . . . [W]hen Paul Bunyan came back from making Europe safe for the democracy of the Big Four, he joined the lumberjack's local to help make the Pacific slope safe for the working-stiffs. The wobblies were reds. Not a thing in this world Paul Bunyan's ascared of.[2]

In 1936, Carl Sandburg devoted a canto of *The People, Yes* to an investigation of the appeal of this populist hero. The brave Paul Bunyan of *Nineteen Nineteen* had been an emblematic figure, a heroic individual, the one who stood for the unionized many. The many, of course, were Sandburg's titular heroes. So while he dutifully recounted the myth of "The Winter of Blue Snow," delineating Bunyan in all his singularity—his gargantuan flapjacks, his titanic dinner table, his various bulky mascots, his off-season campaigns against a species of monstrous mosquito—Sandburg cared less for the unique protagonist of the stories than for their smalltown storytellers.

"Who Made Paul Bunyan?" asked the poet, in a grand rhetorical flourish. Who invented a woodland hero mighty enough to challenge the wintery wrath of nature itself? "The people" did, he declared.[3] The anonymous folk concocted Paul Bunyan out of the genial humor of their collective imagination and their mutual resilience of spirit. The Blue Snow tales were Depression-time parables, fables testifying to the force of the American will. Paul Bunyan got his massive stature from the frontier savvy and the native grit of a nation, from the energy of a whole people endowed with the indomitable legacy of the westering pioneers.[4]

If the Paul Bunyan stories were autobiographical annals of ordinary people who performed herculean feats when challenged by the enormousness of the obstacles before them, then what transpired in northern Minnesota during the bitter winter of 1937 was hardly remarkable. Faced with bad business and worse weather, idle conversation among the story-tellers around the stove turned to practical issues. Despite his Wobbly adventures in Dos Passos's novel, Paul Bunyan, the worker-hero, proved remarkably sympathetic to the cause of commerce in Minnesota. From the congenial chatter of Sandburg's people, a compelling image emerged. As they talked, the myth of Paul Bunyan began to take on the awkward solidity of real life. And so, in the bitter winter of 1937, the people of Bemidji fashioned a colossal statue of Paul Bunyan, and set it up in a snowy field by the side of a road. An immense and intensely blue Babe soon joined his master on the edge of ice-covered Lake Bemidji.

Marking the primary route heading west through town, the glossy red and blue figures invited the motorist to abandon the highway for Bemidji's first annual Paul Bunyan Winter Carnival. These crudely formed, garishly colored behemoths demanded attention by the sheer force of their intrusion upon the flat, white wintertime landscape of Minnesota. And the 15-foot Paul, at least in his early years, attracted notice with awkward, lurching gestures produced by hidden wires, while Babe, sometimes given an eye-catching winter coat of blue flocking, cantered about the site precariously mounted on the chassis of a Model A.[5]

These awkward, gangling monsters were, and are, peculiar enough in their own right to warrant bemused attention, quite apart from their freakish dominance of the empty plains along Route 2. Today, Paul and Babe are almost as intriguing in postcard view, or in a grainy newspaper photograph, as they are in person. The Bemidji Bunyan remains the prototypical midwestern roadside colossus.[6]

The harvest season of 1978 was a scorcher. Undaunted by the heat, the citizens of Blue Earth, Minnesota, on the south-central border of the state, roasted and devoured two hogs and, with the help of the governor, Miss America, Miss Minnesota, and a gaggle of lesser celebrities, dedicated a fifty-foot Jolly Green Giant facing the new stretch of Interstate 90 outside town. September 24, 1978, was, as the *Minneapolis Tribune* noted with

The new Paul Bunyan at Bemidji, ca. 1937. Hakkerup photograph, from the collections of the Minnesota Historical Society.

A mobile Babe, ca. 1938. Hakkerup photograph, from the collections of the Minnesota Historical Society.

The Bemidji ensemble today—a summertime view. Photo by the author.

The Jolly Green Giant in Blue Earth, Minnesota. Photo by the author.

The first Red River Lumber brochure. Illustration by W. B. Laughead.

heavy irony, a day of national significance; with the completion of the last 14 miles of freeway north of Blue Earth, the longest interstate highway in America was finally done, too. Boston and Seattle were linked by a seamless ribbon of concrete, running from Atlantic to Pacific with nary a stoplight. The Jolly Green Giant, just arrived by truck convoy from the Creative Display sculpture factory in Sparta, Wisconsin, became, in effect, an updated version of the transcontinental railroad's "golden spike" of 1869, marking the point where East at last met West. Officials from the U.S. Department of Transportation had, in fact, painted several panels of the highway "a dullish gold" for the occasion, but the historic reference was lost on the town fathers, who paid for the Giant, and on the natives, who turned out in droves to watch him being levered into position. From a local viewpoint, the freeway exchange, where a Dairy Queen, a Country Kitchen, and three motels were in the works, had nothing to offer Blue Earth, unless motorists could be induced to stop short at the feet of the big, green statue:

> . . . if they don't stop in our town, they won't do us any good. That's why we built in [the] Green Giant. We're going to have a nice park there and we hope in the future to build a Little Sprout . . . and put in some giant shoes that kids can sit in. He's high and he's interesting and the real proof will be if people stop in to see him.[7]

Like the Paul Bunyan of 1937, the Jolly Green Giant of 1978 is a resonant mark of local presence, a magnet drawing the traveler off the westward course of history and highway, into the mythical realm of the American Midwest. That mythic Midwest was a communal story, first told in the 1920s, long before it ever became a series of tangible, roadside tableaux, etched in memory by a succession of tourist attractions.

Paul Bunyan tales, as recounted in the free, comical brochures widely distributed by the Red River Lumber Company of Minneapolis in 1922, provided topical chuckles to small-town businessmen for years, and only gradually congealed into the 10-ton mass of polychromed concrete erected in Bemidji in 1937.[8] The Jolly Green Giant was invented in 1925 to serve as a friendly trademark for the sweet peas packed by the Minnesota Valley Canning Company. With national exposure, the Giant developed a biography of sorts in the 1950s and 60s, along with a cheerful personality asserted in cartoon ads on television and in mail-order deals for cuddly rag dolls. Finally, he acquired the attendant "Sprout" that Blue Earth residents, in 1978, so earnestly wished to install beside their 50-foot green fiberglass landmark.[9]

Published in 1925, *The Great Gatsby* is another such midwestern story. The story is also a landmark in literary form: like the ponderous monuments in Blue Earth and Bemidji, it helps to define the essential reality of midwestern space. As the novel opens, Jay Gatsby is dead. Nick Carraway stands on the Long Island shore and looks west, back toward America, back toward the midwestern city of his birth, and back toward the gentle hills of Northfield, Minnesota, where the young Jimmy Gatz, a farmboy from North Dakota, had his first, fatal brush with the canons of high culture, "where the dark fields of the republic rolled on under the night."

The sensibility of F. Scott Fitzgerald, late of St. Paul, Minnesota, and the preoccupations of Nick Carraway, his transplanted, jazz-baby narrator, bear directly on the temporal, the geographic, the spiritual, and the aesthetic dimensions of the American roadside colossus, the popular monument through which the Midwest has, for almost half a century, articulated a sense of regional identity. Like Gatsby himself, these raw, New World colossi possess "a vast, vulgar, and meretricious beauty" symbolic of the American dilemma of the 20th century, and of America's dreams.[10]

A sportsmen's promotional map, featuring Paul Bunyan, published in Duluth, Minnesota, in 1935. *Sports Afield.*

The genial Giant still humanizes the canning industry. This billboard stands above the highway outside Le Sueur, Minnesota, his corporate home. Photo by Liz Harrison.

THE HOAX, THE AD, AND THE FRONTIER   Mythological Giants Arise to Fill the Vastness of the American West

"And as the moon rose higher the inessential houses began to melt away until gradually," Nick recounts,

> I became aware of the old island here that flowered once for Dutch sailors' eyes—a fresh green breast of the new world. Its vanished trees . . . had once pandered in whispers to the last and greatest of all human dreams; for a transitory enchanted moment man must have held his breath in the presence of this continent, compelled into an aesthetic contemplation he neither understood nor desired, face to face for the last time in history with something commensurate to his capacity for wonder.[11]

What compels that wonder is nothing less than a continent, so vast as to be unknowable, beyond all intimacy, of a scale commensurate with nothing save the boundless, intangible limits of the imagination. In 1608, in 1937, and in 1978 Fitzgerald's America responds to the environmental aesthetic of surfeit, gigantism, the colossal—a hugeness perceptible only by the swollen measure of itself. American culture has endlessly contended with the riddle of heroic scale: of how the finite individual can find his bearings in the infinite immensity of space; of how to symbolize and so come to grips with a wholly new world, sized for Titans or for gods.

In the optimism and surety of a Revolution won, painters turned to the weird might of Niagara as their first affirmation of nationhood tenuously imposed upon the sublime and the terrible. The Hudson River romantics sought out the highest peaks, the broadest vistas, be-

Niagara Falls. Photo by the author.

Thomas Cole's *Oxbow* of 1836 typifies the Hudson River School approach to the vast expanse of the American continent. Photo courtesy of the Metropolitan Museum of Art, New York; gift of Mrs. Russell Sage, 1908.

fore which the lilliputian citizen stood awed by the immensity of America, "last and greatest of all human dreams," now come palpably true.[12] The aesthetic of awe spilled over into Charles Willson Peale's Philadelphia museum, where the curtain rose on the American Mastodon, the mightiest, the biggest creature in all of history, an emblem of the stunning magnitude of its native soil, a token of a time as stupendous as the space the mammoth had yielded to man.[13]

The growing conviction that a nature that spawned the Grand Canyon, the Great Lakes, the Rockies, and the trackless sprawl of the Great Plains worked according to different measurements in America provided the climate in which avid exploration, earnest naturalism, and outrageous hoax could flourish apace. For every Audubon and Agassiz, there was a P. T. Barnum, a George Hull. The latter was a peripatetic cigarmaker who, during an otherwise uneventful visit to his brother-in-law in Ackley, Iowa, became fascinated by a preacher's earnest sermonizing on Biblical "giants in the earth in those days," and even more intrigued by the congregation's unquestioning belief in that story from the Book of Genesis. After a decent interval, he brought a slab of gypsum from a quarry in Fort Dodge, Iowa, hired a crew of shady marble cutters in Chicago, and quietly set his plot in motion.[14]

Hull secretly commissioned a grotesque, recumbent effigy of himself, swollen to a height of 10 feet, 4½ inches; shipped it from Chicago to Cardiff, New York; and buried it in a field not too far from Peale's mastodon pit. Then, late one night, Hull dug the statue up, proclaiming loudly that he had found the Cardiff Giant, a petrified American form of humanity indeed commensurate with the aboriginal mass of the continent. In 1869, a peep at the Giant cost 50 cents. Diverted profits sent Barnum into a paroxysm of noctural giant fakery, until public credulousness slowly reached its limits, and Yale paleontologist O. C. Marsh pronounced the petrified fake "a decided humbug." The original Cardiff Giant vanished into the fastness of the heartland, where it popped up at small-time carnies well into the 1930s,

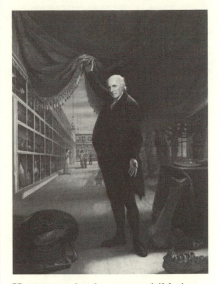

Huge mastodon bones are visible in the right foreground and background of Charles Willson Peale's *The Artist in his Museum* of 1822. Photo courtesy of the Pennsylvania Academy of the Fine Arts, Philadelphia; Joseph and Sarah Harrison Collection.

"The Cardiff Giant—Hoisting the Statue from the Pit," after an original photograph by C. O. Gott. Photo courtesy of Special Collections Library, New York State Historical Association, Cooperstown, New York.

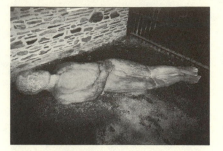

The Cardiff Giant was carved in secret by Fred Mohrmann and Henry Salle. Photo courtesy of New York State Historical Association, Cooperstown, New York.

and was finally rediscovered in a basement rumpus room in Des Moines, Iowa, just after World War II, the oldest and the oddest American colossus to come to rest in Nick Carraway's Midwest.[15]

Implicit in accounts of Hull's "Great American Hoax" is the notion that public naivete does not explain a positive relish for being duped: indeed, if a fraud bolstered local or national pride, its success was virtually assured.[16] Thus cultural historian Neil Harris takes the Cardiff Giant and his kin seriously, as indices of American concerns. Accounting for the prevalence of overblown hoaxes in the "competitive materialism of American life" in the 19th century, Harris confronts the proximity of the frontier and the scale of an untamed, largely uncharted natural world "fraught with obstacles and dangers." The trickster's hoax, he argues, is an artifactual analogue to practical jokes and tall tales, with their boasting and exaggerations. Humor and fakery create situations that appear "dangerous, horrible, or uncanny" and then disperse the sensation of terror with the sudden realization that the whole thing is a hoax. Humbuggery approximates what Freud called " 'anxiety' — the imaginative creation of danger, a psychic exercise designed to reduce the stature of real danger." The hoax survived and thrived in a frontier culture because, like the tall tale, it was a way of diminishing "a hostile and threatening environment to human scale by manipulating its elements and so demonstrating control over them."[17]

Thus, the larger-than-life braggadocio of Mike Fink, King of the Keelboatmen and the Mississippi River frontier, challenging the puny, "milk-white mechanics" of the East to a tussle:

> I'm the very infant that refused his milk before its eyes were open, and called out for a bottle of old rye. . . . I'm half wild horse and half cockeyed alligator and the rest o' me is crooked snags an' red hot snappin' turkle. I can hit like fourth-proof lightenin' an' every lick I make in the woods lets in an acre o' sunshine. I

can outrun, outjump, outshoot, outbrag, outdrink, an' outfight, rough-an'-tumble, no holts barred, ary man on both sides of the river from Pittsburgh to New Orleans an' back agin to St. Louiee.[18]

Hence, too, Mike Fink's inevitable show-down with Davy Crockett, king of the frontier trail, the ring-tailed roarer turned superman, who cured a toothache by biting the tail of a live grizzly bear and carried the sunrise west in the pocket of his buckskins. The rhetoric of Mike Fink and the Crockett Almanack both reveals the perilous immensity of the frontier challenge and inflates the human capacity to vie with it, at a comparable scale. Insofar as these cycles of myth stemmed from the folk tradition, they represent a distilled, collective response to the frontier.[19] And these 19th-century yarns, like the Cardiff Giant, origi-nated at midcontinent, on the margins of a fixed topography, as did the 20th-century myth of Paul Bunyan, the synthetic lumberjack hero of the as yet unmastered forests of Minnesota and the Upper Midwest.

In the canonical version of the legend, Paul Bunyan was an easterner, born in Maine. When he was only three weeks old, the rocking of his cradle toppled four square miles of standing timber. So his cradle was floated out to sea, off Eastport, but the rocking continued and touched off tidal waves. The old, settled East was just too small for Paul Bunyan, and he headed West, with Babe, his big Blue Ox, whose hoofprints carved the Great Lakes. In fact, Paul had to log the Dakotas clean just to make a stall big enough for Babe to lie down in![20]

Paul Bunyan seems every bit as authentic a hero as Davy Crockett, who actually lived and fought at the Alamo. Bunyan's exploits were solemnly memorialized by sculptor William McVey in 1937, in a series of oversized, feder-ally sponsored reliefs adorning a housing proj-ect in Cleveland, Ohio, set above the shores of Lake Erie.[21] And in 1937, Bemidji's giant, roughhewn statues of Paul and Babe intro-duced the roadside colossus to Minnesota and the Midwest. Erected hard by a Chamber of

A woodcut showing a "Fatal Bear Fight on the Banks of the Arkansaw," from *Davy Crockett's Almanack*, 1837. Photo courtesy of National Museum of American Art, the Smithsonian Institution.

1937 relief sculpture showing Paul Bunyan carved by William McVey on the facade of the Community Center of Lakeview Terrace, a public housing project in Cleveland, Ohio. Photo by the author.

The personality of the Bemidji group changes with each fresh paint job. Photo courtesy of State of Minnesota, Department of Economic Development.

Sport, the Reversible Dog. From an illustration by W. B. Laughead.

Paul's gun was once a crucial part of the Lake Bemidji ensemble. Anonymous photograph, from the collections of the Minnesota Historical Society.

Commerce tourist information booth barely containing Bunyan's undershorts, fingernail clippings, and toothbrush, the luridly colored grouping invited envy and emulation. "Whenever there's any doubt about where a great man was born," notes Walter Blair in his commentary on America's comic heroes, "any number of places are likely, through their Chambers of Commerce, to fight for the honor."[22] So it was with Homer, in ancient Greece, and so it was, in modern Minnesota, with Paul Bunyan.

Activated by jealousy, Brainerd, Minnesota – calling itself "Paul Bunyan's Playground" – got up a competing Bunyan festival, and late in the 1930s published a promotional folder for vacationing sportsmen containing several new tales of Paul's adventures in the immediate neighborhood. According to Brainerd's hucksters, it was there that Paul met Sport, his "reversible dog," a peerless hunter. Sport was an odd-looking cuss: his hind legs pointed straight up. But that mutt "learned to run on one pair of legs for a while and then flop over without any loss of speed and run on the other pair. Because of this he never got tired and anything he started after got caught."[23] And it was in Brainerd, too, that Paul invented his famous "three-barrel gun"; why, that rifle bagged the really big birds, flying up high in the stratosphere, and the shots sounded like claps of thunder.[24]

There matters stood until 1949: Brainerd had a corner on Bunyanesque fish stories – the one that got away in this neck-of-the-woods was truly awesome! – but Bemidji had those big statues, statues so famous that *Life* magazine had even printed a picture of them. Then Sherman Levis and Roy Kuehmichel, ardent Brainerd boosters, attended a railroad exposition in Chicago where they discovered, ensconced in the display of the Chicago & Northern Railway Company, "the largest animated man in the world," a moveable Paul Bunyan some 36 feet tall, weighing 5,000 pounds. They bought him on the spot.[25] And, in the summer of 1950, Brainerd coaxed motorists to stop and hear this Bunyan – vastly superior, of course, to its deposed rival up north, and localized by the addition of a concrete "Sport, the Reversible

Paul Bunyan Center, Brainerd, Minnesota, ca. 1950. Note "Henry," the giant squirrel, in the foreground, and Sport, to the left of the stage. Anonymous photograph, from the collections of the Minnesota Historical Society.

Dog" to a growing collection of subsidiary curiosities—tell tall tales with his own mechanical lips:

> [Paul] talks, tells stories and sings in lumberjack style. His size 44 cap shades his 16" moveable blue eyes. His broad shoulders and long 18 ft. arms are protected by a size 73 shirt, which consists of 60 yards of wool-plaid material. Paul wears a size 80 boot with soles 5 feet long. This is a true mechanical figure of the legendary Minnesota's Paul Bunyan.[26]

The battle of the giants commenced. Bemidji touted a free Bunyan exhibit that included such intimate relics of the hero as his toothpaste, straight razor, telephone, zippo lighter, watch, and wallet. In Hackensack, unruly kids were silenced by a glimpse of Paul's amazonian sweetheart, the fetching Miss LucetteDiana Kensack. His cradle went on display at Akeley, while its anchor was marooned at Ortonville; meanwhile, a specimen of his stratospheric quarry, in cement replica, became the eponymous mascot of Blackduck, Minnesota. A

The levers visible here allow Paul to blink, raise his hand, and nod his head as he talks to guests. Anonymous photograph, from the collections of the Minnesota Historical Society.

Paul has undergone a facelift in recent years and wears a new shirt. Photo by the author.

massive three-barrel gun was also supplied. Brainerd fired back with a new Paul Bunyan phone, and with a Babe of unparalleled ferocity and blinding blueness. But Kelliher carried the day with a grassy mound, some 40 feet in length, tucked in a shady corner of the town park. At one end, wreathed in flowers, lay a marble tablet inscribed thus:

PAUL BUNYAN
1794 to 1899
Here lies Paul, and that's all.[27]

Paul Bunyan, his retinue and his cyclopean accessories were not the detritus of an ancient folk tradition, but the shiny byproducts of

This ax is among the giant accessories at Brainerd. Photo by the author.

Other accessories include the giant mushrooms dotted about the miniature golf course adjacent to Paul's lair. Note the little bridges and the tiny water wheel on the eighteenth hole. Photo by the author.

Paul Bunyan's cradle in Akeley, Minnesota. Photo by Liz Harrison.

LucetteDiana Kensack, Paul's Hackensack, Minnesota, sweetheart, once directed tourists north and south via the Bunyan statues in Bemidji and Brainerd. E. D. Becker photograph, from the collections of the Minnesota Historical Society.

A trapdoor, hidden in the rear of her ever-billowing skirt, is an intriguing feature of the statue. Photo by Liz Harrison.

Miss Kensack's allure varies considerably, with the quality of the annual paint job. Photo courtesy of State of Minnesota, Department of Economic Development.

Paul's boat anchor, in Ortonville.
Photo by the author.

His duck—slightly the worse for
wear—in Blackduck, Minnesota.
These figures came from Bemidji.
Photo by Liz Harrison.

Babe in Brainerd, in the parking lot
outside the Paul Bunyan Center.
Photo by the author.

modern, jazz-age advertising — of popular, mass culture. Stories lumberjacks told and other bits of forest apocrypha began to form a coherent mythology in 1910, when James MacGillivray, a newspaper man and former logger, set down reminiscences of his youth in the logging camps. Between 1914 and 1922, W. B. Laughead, an advertising copywriter based in Minneapolis, gradually made one Paul Bunyan the protagonist of all such stories, added humorous illustrations, and used his new creation to promote the products of the Red River Lumber Company of Minnesota.[28] Early booklets were modest affairs, of postcard size. By 1924, the third edition of *The Marvelous Exploits of Paul Bunyan*, "published for the amusement of [the] friends" of the firm, ran to forty folio pages with a handsome hardboard cover and a preface stressing the association between Laughead's genial, chubby hero and a quality consumer product:

> Paul Bunyan's picture had never been published until he joined Red River and this likeness, first issued in 1914 is now the Red River trademark. It stands for the quality and service you have the right to expect from Paul Bunyan.[29]

Written in a business lingo appealing to his readership of lumber wholesalers, Laughead's stories were ideally suited to the task of attracting city fellows to outstate resorts for camping, hunting, and fishing. Thus it was Laughead himself who concocted the brochure of recreational Bunyan lore circulated by Brainerd's civic chauvinists in support of their brand-new summer tourist festival.[30] A rustic Superman turned supersalesman, Paul Bunyan spoke a language not unlike the Boosters' Club patois favored by *Babbitt*, titular hero of Sinclair Lewis's 1922 novel. George Babbitt, of Zenith, Minnesota, thrived on "heart-to-heart-talk advertisements, 'sales-pulling' letters . . . and hand-shaking house-organs . . . richly poured forth by the new school of Poets of Business."[31] As a vacationer, Babbitt craved the outdoor life. "He treasured every grease spot and fish-scale on his new khaki trousers," al-

TRADE MARK

REGISTERED

The Paul Bunyan trademark of the Red River Lumber Company, designed by W. B. Laughead in 1922. From a design by W. B. Laughead.

Paul, as he appeared in 1924. From an illustration by W. B. Laughead.

though sleeping late and forgetting to shave were preferable to more vigorous activities. As a businessman, Babbitt espoused the gospel of "service." His fortnightly form letter, mimeographed and sent to a thousand hot real estate prospects, concluded with the tag line, "Yours for service": Lewis's advertising parody came wickedly close to the tenor of Paul Bunyan's trademark pledge of "quality and service."[32]

As advertisement, or modern hoax, congealed into legitimate popular myth in Bemidji's astounding sculptural ensemble, so too myth once more became full-color advertisement, a magnet for any transient commerce that might quicken the stagnant economy of backwoods Minnesota in the throes of the Great Depression.[33]

The Bemidji Bunyan suggests that profit and place are the abiding constants uniting the American approach to symbolic scale over two centuries. The Cardiff Giant of 1869 is bracketed by the earlier Crockett Almanacks that sold in the millions and the later Beadle dime-novels that displaced them.[34] All these material and literary embodiments of the gigantic—all these hoaxes, these wild-eyed extrusions of mundane reality—are, in some fashion, commercial phenomena. Peale charged fees for a look at the mastodon. Gypsum giants and their ilk made Barnum rich. Ned Buntline made the manufacture of tall stories into a major industry, whose inventory included a Buffalo Bill legend so bloated as to dwarf William Cody. The narrative version of Paul Bunyan sold lumber in 1922. The sculptural version stopped the unwary traveler and opened his wallet in hard times. Paul Bunyan is, therefore, a commercial colossus of the 20th century, conceived in the spirit of a grand American tradition.

Paul's tombstone in Kelliher, Minnesota. Photo by Liz Harrison.

ANXIETY, NOSTALGIA, AND WORLD'S FAIRS
Colossi Mark the Borders of a Modern America

The literature of the crude, instinctual colossus appealed to an urban audience by virtue of exoticism and, perhaps, fanciful nostalgia, the implicit contrast between the American Adam and the cosseted society that craved word of his untrammeled exploits.[35] The giant was always a significant other, from another kind of place. The monstrous mountains and waterfalls of the Hudson River School stood at a point of geographic remove from the Broadway galleries and the neat, neoclassical parlors where the paintings were much exclaimed over. Such paintings pictured the upstate frontier of Fenimore Cooper and Natty Bumppo, a place out there where nature and the unknown still held sway, despite the challenge of Clinton's Big Ditch. It was here, or rather, just out there, that Peale found his primordial beast. And having concocted his hoax at the threshold of another, later frontier, shifting relentlessly westward, it was to this plausibly symbolic point that George Hull returned to bury his giant.

In 1869, the scale of the frontier called for giants: on that score, show business charlatans and sober practitioners of the fine arts concurred. After mid-century, it was to the western frontier that artist-explorers repaired in their search for "the sublime," for a primal America untouched since it left the hands of the Creator, for a blessed place of great natural antiquity, putting the sordid history of the Old World to shame.[36] The Adamic painter-hero made the scale of Yosemite, the Grand Canyon, and Pike's Peak the chief protagonist in heroic visual dramas that reenacted the popular melodrama staged by George Hull in Stub Newell's Cardiff farmyard. Albert Bierstadt's flamboyant panoramas of the Rockies not only magnified the bulk of those lofty crags, but did so in lurid canvases that themselves routinely attained environmental dimensions. His much-acclaimed, eye-popping vision of the *Domes of the Yosemite*, for instance, measures some 15 feet across by nearly 10 feet in height.[37]

The vast, "official" oils of Bierstadt, Thomas Moran, Thomas Hill, and their contemporaries were destined for public places, of course, after public exhibitions often mounted like theatrical spectacles. Yet so avid was a mass audience for a glimpse of the vanishing frontier paradise that cheap prints of western views multiplied, despite their rather modest plate measurements. The last Moran retrospective of the 19th century was an exhibition of Louis Prang's commercial chromolithographs after the artist's watercolors, presented at the World's Columbian Exposition in Chicago in 1893.[38]

Only among the cognoscenti did rabid enthusiasm for works with western themes begin to wane as the Columbian Exposition approached. From 1863 through 1888, Bierstadt had worked on the picture he conceived as his apotheosis. *The Last of the Buffalo* was a nostalgic portrait of the end of an era. On a vast, desolate plain, the straggling remnant of the once-mighty herd is attacked by the few surviving Indian hunters, above a telling frieze of sun-bleached bones.[39] The American selection committee for the 1889 Paris Exposition rejected *Last of the Buffalo* on stylistic grounds: meticulous realism was sadly out of step with ascendant Impressionism. Nevertheless, the pathetic, retrospective theme of the painting, as well as Bierstadt's interest in the spreading plains that painter-explorers neglected in their rush to the aberrant terrain of the far West, set the elegiac tone and the immoderate scale favored by the artists who built the great frontier fairs of the turn of the century.

In 1882, Walt Whitman anticipated and celebrated Bierstadt's new, level landscape of mid-America:

[W]hile I know the standard claim is that Yosemite, Niagara Falls, the upper Yellowstone and the like, afford the greatest

Albert Bierstadt's *The Last of the Buffalo* of 1888 depicts the flat expanse of the West rather than the towering mountains and bottomless canyons generally favored by his later 19th-century peers. Photo courtesy of the Corcoran Gallery of Art, Washington, D. C.; gift of Mrs. Albert Bierstadt.

natural shows, I am not sure but that the prairies and plains, while less stunning at first sight, last longer, fill the esthetic sense fuller, precede all the rest, and make North America's characteristic landscape. . . . What most impressed me, and will longest remain with me, are these same prairies. Day after day, and night after night, to my eyes, to all my senses—the esthetic one most of all—they silently and broadly unfolded. Even their simplest statistics are sublime.[40]

The sublimity of horizontal extension presented both an aesthetic and a spiritual challenge to the designers of the Columbian Exposition of 1893 and the St. Louis World's Fair— the Louisiana Purchase Exposition—of 1904. The 1893 meeting of the American Historical Association, held in Chicago, coincided with the run of the fair, and before that august body, Frederick Jackson Turner unveiled his epochal frontier thesis. The open land, Turner maintained, had shaped the democratic institutions of the nation. Now, according to data gathered in the 1890 census, that frontier was finally and forever closed. Could America survive the transformation of a frontier culture into the urbanized, mechanized society apparently heralded by Chicago's exuberant displays of native manufactures?

An aching sense of loss – the sense of standing at a watershed where the values of the past were dying but the shape of the future was not yet clear – links Turner to Bierstadt. But even as Turner spoke, Buffalo Bill's enormously popular Wild West show was reducing the Chinese Theatre, the Lapland encampment, and the mounted "Wild East" bedouins to the status of minor side-show attractions on the Midway Plaisance.[41] Cody had founded his troop in 1883 in response to popular demand. His "Old Glory Blowout," a kind of embryonic rodeo held in Nebraska in 1882, drew more than a thousand competitors to North Platte on the Fourth of July to perform for sport and for pleasure tasks no longer required on the shrinking range.[42] Likewise, in 1893, Buffalo Bill's Wild West show was recreating, as theatrical ritual, that last frontier the passage of which Turner noted with trepidation. In 1893, the frontier was a make-believe, cowboy-and-Indian adventure, already consigned to the realm of myth. But Chicago's constant evocation of the myth measures the degree of cultural anxiety associated with the transition from raw frontier to modern city, from pioneer self-reliance to urban interdependence, from America's humble origins to a glittering future symbolized by the tonal purity and dazzle of "the White City" itself.

The Columbian Exposition honored American progress since the days of Columbus, and progress implied a readiness to slough off the impediments of history. But fairgoers' unease over the leap into an uncharted tomorrow was recognized, accommodated, and soothed at all points by the very fabric of the exposition. By and large, the official buildings on the grounds recapitulated architectural conventions from the Renaissance and the ancient world, albeit at a scale unknown before the epoch of iron and steel: the constituent elements were commonplace if the whole, breathtaking snowy-white ensemble was not. Some structures, however, were radical departures from the prevailing

schema, and as such, dramatized cultural anomalies too blatant to be shoehorned into conformity with the millennial purity of tall, white columns. Such was the so-called "Hunter's Cabin." On the "Wooded Island" at the edge of the Chicago fairgrounds stood "a log house with clay floor and stick chimney . . . built by Theodore Roosevelt, of New York, a lover of huntsman's sports, as a museum" in honor of Daniel Boone and Davy Crockett, legendary frontiersmen:

> To complete this picture, a hunter in long hair and wide-brimmed felt hat made his home in the cabin and answered the questions of many visitors, for there was a charm about the premises, pioneers loving to recall the vanished days, and younger inquirers seeming pleased to see before them the picture so often drawn in the tales of their grandsires and this chapter of their romances. Between the Hunter's Cabin and Marie Antoinette's bed chamber in the French section was a wide divergence.[43]

The guidebook caption describing T. R.'s cabin exudes a palpable nostalgia for the good old days, left behind with the 1890 census, and for the frontier that once set a virtuous, natural America apart from the tarnished artifice of Europe. Yet Roosevelt's shrine to Boone and Crockett is also a self-consciously modern environment. Log cabin nostalgia is enjoyable only because the daydreamer is under no real compulsion to live permanently in a drafty shack with clay floors and a stick chimney; the cabin is a sportsman's vacation lair, where frontier ways are not practiced out of necessity but emulated ceremonially, for the pleasure of playacting. The 1893 American—like George Babbitt returning from a fishing resort in 1922—could walk away from the Wild West show and the Hunter's Cabin and resume a modern life.

In everyday life, moments of change from old mores to new ways are trying, because the future outcome of the alteration cannot be predicted with much accuracy. In reality, the

clock cannot be turned back, but in imagination it is possible to savor the past without giving up the comforts of a familiar present or the promise of the future. The principal delight of the White City in Jackson Park was imaginative: the fairgoer had the chance, in recreational fantasy at any rate, to waft over the dangerous boundary between yesterday and tomorrow. At the Fair, it was possible to rehearse that perilous shift from the frontier era to the future in perfect safety. In a sense, then, the Chicago World's Fair, with its western artifacts, constituted a frontier in its own right — a temporal frontier, standing between the city's past as a raucous, frontier railhead for the West, destroyed in the Great Fire of 1871, and the city's future as a trading and commercial center identified by the man-made forest of skyscrapers rising on the shores of Lake Michigan.

The Columbian Exposition of 1893 ostensibly honored the discovery of the western border of the known world by Christopher Columbus: all of America was the frontier in 1492. In fact, it was the rapidly retreating woods, rangeland, and prairie west of Chicago that the frontier imagery of the Fair commemorated. Huge statues of bison and elk, bear, and moose, designed by Edward Kemeys and Phimister Proctor, stood in pairs, gravely guarding the bridges that linked the fairgrounds with the streets of the city. Like the dwindling herds in Bierstadt's *Last of the Buffalo*, these giant effigies were metaphors for the passing away of the American frontier: art preserved in pallid likeness what progress had destroyed.[44] Poised on tall plinths at salient points of entry to the islands upon which stood the principal exhibition buildings, frontier animals articulated places where the pedestrian moved from one order of experience to another. Thus, by virtue of scale, these wildlife sentinels — more than 50 such sculptures were disposed around the edges of the islands and lagoons that dotted the site — made the historical watershed betokened by the fair as a whole into a real frontier, a perimeter sharply drawn between the city and Jackson Park.

The height and bulk of the plaster buffal

Moose Bridge at the Chicago Fair of 1893. Note the huge, Renaissance-style exposition buildings in the background. From an original photograph by the N. D. Thompson Publishing Company, St. Louis, Missouri.

keeping watch over the so-called "Farmers' Bridge" to the Grand Basin made the route and the journey along it both memorable and immediately consequential. Pictorial guidebooks to the 1893 Fair devoted whole pages to "Moose Bridge," "Farmers' Bridge," and the rest, and squandered whole paragraphs of text on descriptions of the topographic features simultaneously conjoined and differentiated by the sculpted approachways.[45] Such creatures still flank the highways of the Midwest, and words are still unequal to the task of explaining their presence. Today's guidebooks are hazy, for instance, on why "the world's largest buffalo," a concrete monster some 26 feet high, has stood by the side of the road in Jamestown, North Dakota, since 1958, courtesy of a series of costly appropriations by the city council. The state Travel Division says that the three-story buffalo is a monument, "a reminder of the huge herds that once roamed the prairies." It is a monument, to be sure, and a tourist come-on for Frontier Village, just up the street. But it is also a stupendous place marker, a landmark setting this place on the prairie apart from all others.[46] The volumetric mass of the 60-ton buffalo competes successfully with the flat landscape around it to define a special place, the spot where the old frontier of the bison and the pioneer once began.

In 1893, colossal scale and frontier theme combined to produce a similar effect "on the borders of the western lagoon" near the entrance to the Transportation Building at the World's Fair, where two large equestrian groups by Proctor depicted *The Cowboy* and *The Indian*. The *Chicago Record* noted that Proctor and Kemeys, whose primary task had been to ornament the nodal bridges and balustrades controlling pedestrian comprehension of space, distance, and direction, "have come to their exact knowledge of the shape of American wild animals by following the hunter's life in order to learn their art." Like the buffalo and the bear, moreover, Proctor's Indian was based on careful observation:

One of Buffalo Bill's Indians—Red Cloud—was the sculptor's model. He

The "World's Largest Buffalo," at the Frontier Village in Jamestown, North Dakota. Ken Jorgensen photograph, courtesy of North Dakota Travel Division.

Proctor's colossal Indian. Its companion piece, a giant Cowboy, can be glimpsed at the right, beneath the pony's hind leg. From an original photograph by the N. D. Thompson Publishing Company, St. Louis, Missouri.

became very much interested in the work and posed on his pony in all sorts of positions. The attitude finally chosen is one of rest, but the expression is one of intense eagerness and repressed action. The Indian puts his hand over his eyes and intently gazes across the plains to the far horizon, seeking his foe.[47]

Formulated in the wings of the Wild West show, this image of the frontier is a popular one. It inflates the strength of the white cowboy-conquerer of the plains as well as the menace of his nemesis, the Indian. It inflates the immensity of the frontier, too. And it reflects the magnitude of the loss felt by Americans in 1893, with the disappearance of a West whose distant horizon in the recesses of history, on the plains of time, only the sculpted eyes of art can still perceive.

Heroic scale calls attention to the inherently theatrical and dynamic character of the American Dream of a frontier without limits of time or space. Great size comes to stand for America, and size *per se* becomes synonymous with American superiority. As *The Republic* was personified by "the central statuary of the Fair" – Daniel Chester French's gilded, 65-foot figure of a goddess crowned in laurel – America was a massive presence that rivaled and surpassed all the wonders of the known world:

The ancients delighted in heroic statues, such as the Colossus of Rhodes, the Egyptian Sphinx . . . and the statues of Jupiter at Athens and Olympus, which made the fame of Phidias. But the moderns, until the day of Bartholdi, did not undertake great effigies, and the success of Daniel C. French . . . was owing to the general resemblance of his figure to humanity, and not because it offered a model of form or fashion. Indeed, it is impossible to determine whether the figure is too short or too tall, as the judgment will surely be formed according to the distance of the eye from the pedestal. . . . When it came to the gilding of the statue – for it appears as a golden

The centerpiece of the 1893 Fair, *The Republic* by Daniel Chester French, deliberately rivaled the Sphinx and the Colossus of Rhodes in scale and pomp. From an original photograph by the N. D. Thompson Publishing Company, St. Louis, Missouri.

image, after the methods of Phidias—it was found that no less than $1,400 worth of gold-leaf was required for the labor. The total cost was about $25,000. The face is fifteen feet long, the little fingers a yard. The total height from the water is one hundred feet.[48]

In actual size, then, *The Republic* was a finite marvel, designed according to certain measurements, at a certain cost. But in scale, determined solely by the eye of the beholder, *The Republic* could be as infinite as the dimensions of the American Dream.

As the new century began, only colossal size could match the vaunting ambition of a rising generation of American sculptors from the West. Their leader was Lorado Taft, who had emerged from the studios of the Columbian Exposition as a zealous proselytizer for public art, the premier public sculptor of the Midwest, and its leading exponent of monumentality. The heady rivalry between Daniel Chester French and Phidias had not been lost on young Taft: he was acutely aware of the cultural distance that yawned between modern-day Illinois and ancient Athens.[49] "I think that if there is anything America needs," he allowed in one of his entertaining chalk-talks, "it is a sense of the sequence of things. In Europe, everything speaks of a past age; we Americans live casually like the grasshoppers. We have forgotten our forebears as they never do across the sea."[50]

In Illinois, the short "sequence of things" led directly to the conquest of the frontier. Since 1898, a group of prominent Chicago artists and thinkers had been repairing to Eagle's Nest Bluff, near Oregon, Illinois, for a summer "camp" in the out-of-doors. There Lorado Taft discovered that if nature was the American alternative to history, what wilderness remained bespoke a native antiquity worthy of resurrection. Specifically, Taft and his friends came upon the autobiography of Chief Black Hawk of the Sac-Fox, who had made his last, desperate stand for the valley of the Mississippi in 1832 within the precincts of their rustic retreat. In the imagination of the vacationers, a noble, brooding presence haunted

Black Hawk, a 48-foot statue in reinforced concrete by Lorado Taft, was inspired by the large-scale sculpture of the Chicago Fair. From an etching by Thomas Wood Stevens (1911).

the spot where the destiny of a nation had once demanded a bitter choice:

> Here could be either the solitary hunting ground *or* all-invading cities; the fishing pool *or* the factory site; the prairie game pasture *or* the cultivated farm; the lone tepee *or* crowded skyscrapers; the trail *or* the railroad—but not both.[51]

Progress won out, but, as Hamlin Garland noted in an original poem read at the dedication of Taft's colossal statue of Black Hawk in July of 1911, without the deeds of the vanquished, the history of the victors would be dry and thin:

And so today, free from all hate and dread,
    Here, midway of the land they fought to save
We meet in tribute of the storied dead,
    Whose ashes mingle in a common grave.
To him who died in exile, chieftain still,
    A victim of our greed, with broken heart,
We raise this sentinel of the hill,
    This splendid symbol of remorseful Art.[52]

That sentinel was a 48-foot statue, mounted on a limestone bluff rising 200 feet above the Rock River. *Black Hawk* was a symbol of national antiquity. Its columnar form, however, betrayed divided loyalties to the caryatids of the ancient world and to the technology of 20th-century America. The sculptor called *Black Hawk* "our Colossus," reviving the ancient usage, but it is ironic that Taft's monument to tradition was found noteworthy in 1911 and for years thereafter chiefly because of the modern methods used in its fabrication. *Black Hawk* was known as "the largest reinforced concrete statue in the world": his lofty eminence was derived from the shape of a Chicago smokestack under construction.[53]

In the end, *Black Hawk* honored the sentiments and sensibility of a modern Chicago. The towering size of Taft's Indian paid tangible homage to the magnitude of the obstacles overcome by the ancestors of those who solemnly unveiled the statue. By honoring their forebears, the artistic elite of the Middle West exalted their own sturdy virtues. The looming bulk of *Black Hawk* served as what Garland called a "Trail Marker," identifying their own highly civilized haunts as the once-upon-a-time American frontier, "midway of the land"; by raising a landmark above the farms and factories, above the cities and skyscrapers and railroads of their bustling new world, modern midwesterners congratulated themselves on their incredible accomplishments.

It is small wonder, then, that the Louisiana Purchase Exposition of 1904 and the Panama-Pacific Exposition of 1915 featured similar colossi with frontier themes, for both of these civic festivals were awash in self-congratulations. The St. Louis World's Fair aimed to amass proof of a century of unalloyed progress on the midwestern frontier, in aid of which the marvels of science and industry were displayed cheek by jowl with a gigantic plaster enlargement of a statuette by Frederic Remington variously dubbed *Cowboys Shooting Up a Western Town, Off the Trail*, or *Comin' Through the Rye*. In fact, the heroic ensemble stood on the boundary between the cluster of dignified "palaces" devoted to manufactures, machinery, varied industries, and metallurgy, and the amusement zone, a midway known in St. Louis as "The Pike." The placement of the statue was applauded in the official guidebook to the attractions:

> This striking group stands as an appropriate introduction to the Pike, suggesting the spirit of fun and revelry that marks that wonderful street. Mr. Remington, who designed this vigorous and lifelike work, put into it the western spirit that animates his paintings. . . . The cowboys have tired of the work of the ranch and the trail, and have ridden like a whirlwind into some small town, shooting and yelling, terrorizing the timid, but with no real intent to do harm. . . . If someone should be hit by a bullet, it is merely one of the accidents of the game. If the play should be a little rougher than usual, some daring but unimaginative officer of the law may capture the roisterers, but ordinarily they go as they come, and the town resumes its customary quiet.[54]

Remington's colossal cowboys at the entrance to the midway of the St. Louis Fair, 1904. From an original photograph by the Official Photographic Company, St. Louis, Missouri.

The border between The Pike and the Plaza of St. Louis, around which the material signs of progress were proudly ranged, functioned as frontier dividing the present from a cowboy past. In 1904, the motif of wranglers hoorahing some outpost of civilization after weeks on the trail was already a staple ingredient of the western legend Remington purveyed in illustrated articles for *Harper's Weekly* and *Collier's*.[55] It was a story, a diversion, an amusement suitable for The Pike but not, perhaps, serious or consequential enough for The Plaza. St. Louis had long since passed over that raw frontier into civilized, industrious modernity.

In 1804, St. Louis was the gateway to a frontier that ended in California; in 1904, thanks to the Panama Canal, manifest destiny encompassed the Pacific. Originally, the San Francisco Fair had been planned as a modest celebration of the opening of the Canal. After the calamitous earthquake of 1906, however, the Fair became "a bold display to tourists and potential investors of San Francisco's recovery from disaster. The rebuilding of San Francisco and the construction of the Panama Canal were hailed as twin achievements of Herculean proportions."[56] A giant Hercules graced the exposition's official poster; a colossal Indian warrior, slumped dejectedly over the back of his pony facing the sea, won a gold medal for sculpture at San Francisco and became the most popular statue of the 20th century.[57]

The End of the Trail had a protracted gestation period. Sculptor James Earle Fraser had been born in Winona, Minnesota, in 1876, and despite a smattering of schooling in Minneapolis and Chicago, was an authentic frontiersman who grew up in the Black Hills of South Dakota. In those days, the territory was still a wilderness: "Living in a box car, . . . sleeping on the floor wrapped in painted Indian buffalo skins, [he] knew the blizzards and rigors of prairie weather and the hazards of pioneer life."[58] When the aspiring artist made the mandatory trip to Paris at the age of 19, he carried with him a rough model of *End of the Trail*, a reflection of his boyhood memories, to be sure, but a work of art directly inspired by Proctor's colossal Indian at the Columbian Exposition.

James Earle Fraser's *End of the Trail*, created for the Panama-Pacific International Exposition of 1915. Photo courtesy of the National Cowboy Hall of Fame and Western Heritage Center, Oklahoma City, Oklahoma.

The little model, in turn, became the inspiration for the heroic *Cheyenne Chief*, Fraser's own equestrian Indian at the St. Louis World's Fair. The St. Louis figure, enlarged to three times life size and crumpled over his shield, became San Francisco's *End of the Trail* in 1915.

The centerpiece of the Panama-Pacific Exposition was the Court of the Universe, a plaza approached from either end through colossal archways symbolizing the Orient and the Americas, united by the Canal. Atop the arches, more than 150 feet in the air, perched monumental statuary representing the nations of the East (a brace of elephants) and the West (a covered wagon, predictably enough). Fraser's huge Indian occupied no such position of prominence; tucked away in an alcove off the Court of Peace, *End of the Trail* was virtually invisible in the hand-tinted plates of souvenir view-books.[59]

Nonetheless, photographs of the the statue were canonical exposition keepsakes. In 1915, receipts from the sale of pictures reached $150,000 and the fame of the motif grew.[60] By 1920, in the absence of copyright, over 200,000 photographic prints had been sold, and the photographs had evolved into garish chromo-lithographs for calendars that also bore saccharine verses on mortality. Many admirers of *End of the Trail* believed it to be a "famous picture," in incandescent color, until entrepreneurs began to produce sculptural versions in pseudo-bronze relief, attached to ash trays and bookends. The attitude of defeat, aped by a living rider, even became the trademark finale for the rodeo; it was widely reported that a Seneca chief, John Big Tree, struck the pose for Fraser during the summer of 1912 between the acts of a Wild West show on Coney Island.[61]

As the pirated Indians multiplied, *End of the Trail* lost all association with Fraser, whose subsequent reputation hinged on his design for the equally beloved five-cent piece of 1913 issue, the Buffalo Nickel. In part, the autogenous character of the figure arose from the vicissitudes suffered by the Panama-Pacific version of the statue. When the Exposition closed, the managers sold the original stucco piece outright to the city of Visalia, California.

For all intents and purposes, the statue, like the old West of the Indian, disappeared. Although he had realized not one Buffalo Nickel from the sales of various reproductions, the popularity of the motif gave Fraser reason to hope that the public would demand, and subsidize, a colossal version in durable materials for a more visible and meaningful site. "It has seemed to strike a popular note of sympathy," he wrote, adding dryly that the souvenir-hawkers of San Francisco, in 1915 alone, "made far more than it would have cost to erect the statue permanently."[62] He envisioned a great, bronze rider poised on the Pacific Palisades, giving witness to the literal finale of the frontier and marking the western terminus of the Lincoln Highway:

> It has been a dream of mine to erect this horse and rider in permanent form on some bold promontory just outside San Francisco, and on the very edge of the Pacific. There they would stand forever looking out on the waste of waters—with nought save the precipice and the ocean before them—driven at last to the very edge of the continent. That would be, in very truth, *The End of the Trail.*[63]

What Bierstadt, Proctor, Taft, and the others had dimly sensed, James Earle Fraser saw with a startling but unavailing clarity: insofar as the distant edges of the American landscape represented memorable junctures in human affairs, the frontier called for the same titanic scale in monuments that it had always demanded in ambitions and dreams, in stories and lies. And the liminal aesthetic of the frontier also dictated its own, peculiar iconography. Like the statuary, the landscape paintings, the natural wonders, and the ersatz marvels—like *The End of the Trail*, *The Last of the Buffalo*, Niagara, and the Cardiff Giant—the popular, heroic mythology of Mike Fink, Davy Crockett, Buffalo Bill and, finally, Paul Bunyan, arose from and adhered to this mobile point of demarcation between known and unknown, cosmos and chaos, actuality and imagination. The native colossus, reclaiming its antique function, bestrode the psychic boundary line that is the elusive and eternal American frontier.

FRONTIERS, HIGHWAYS, AND MINIATURE GOLF
The Tourist Becomes a Roadside Colossus

The Colossus at Rhodes once separated Greek from barbarian, civilization from the terrors of the wine-dark sea. The Sphinx posed the conundrum of life at the border between the realms of the quick and the dead.[64] These wonders of the ancient world were wondrous because of their dazzling size but were more wondrous still by virtue of their placement at salient gateways, dividing one order of reality from another. The place itself was a locus of wonderment, revelation, and enchantment where, "for a transitory enchanted moment man must have held his breath" and paused. The colossus is a stele that points not to itself alone but to a place of passage. It is a landmark demanding hiatus and awe, at a sacral point of transition.[65]

In the first century A.D., Pliny the Elder gave the term final definition when he described "enormously huge statues . . . called Colossi, as large as towers." Until construction of the gigantic statue of Helios at Rhodes in 204 B.C., however, a colossus was not merely, or only, a big statue. A colossus could be a little statuette housing the spiritual essence of a participant in magic ritual, or any sculpture with a distinctive columnar shape.[66] Magical and "herm"-like properties continued to adhere to large statuary, Pliny's simplistic exegesis notwithstanding.

The square, tapering pillars called "herms" by the Greeks were named for the god Hermes, the messenger who conducted the souls of the dead to the underworld, and thus the patron of all travelers. His was the spirit resident in the piles of stones heaped up along the roadsides as signposts or landmarks for passersby. The Romans dubbed such columns "terms," after Terminus, their god of boundaries: the phallic

An 18th-century reconstruction of the ancient statue of Helios, astride the entrance to the harbor at Rhodes: the Colossus of Rhodes. From J. B. Fisher von Erlach, *Historische Architektur* (1721).

thrust of the cairn not only defined a route for the wayfarer through otherwise featureless terrain but also asserted possession of the land beyond the borders of the road. In the Middle Ages, the sense of place and ownership inherent in the herm, along with a hint of magical power, became firmly associated with large-scale statuary. Medieval folklore and festivals depicted founder-champions of towns as giants, in a convention that signified mighty deeds through immense physical stature. The protective magic of the tutelary giant, a benevolent *genius loci*, passed to its colossal, sculptural image and, in the Renaissance, that apotropaic power trickled down to the ruler or the state commissioning a massive triumphal arch surmounted by a quadriga, a fountain bedecked with ample figures modeled after the antique, a colossus emblematic of civic *virtu*.[67] The technical difficulty and the expense of erecting such grandiose images as Michelangelo's huge Florentine *David* made for ready associations with real and with superhuman powers.

On the authority of Latin texts, Cellini decreed that a colossus should be three times life size. When Michelangelo, after much study of the question, planned a figure of Jupiter to occupy the site of that deity's old shrine on the Capitoline Hill, he took exception to Cellini's rule, judging a height of 16 feet quite sufficient to rival the glories of old Rome. Virginia Bush's study of colossal sculpture of the Cinquecento makes it clear that Renaissance artists approached the creation of oversize works with the example of antiquity firmly in mind. Of the Seven Wonders of the World commonly listed in the 16th century, three (four, by some counts) were ancient colossi. From ancient texts, the Renaissance also knew the story of Deinocrates's mad proposal to carve Mount Athos into a statue of Alexander the Great, holding a city of 10,000 in one hand and in the other, a bowl spewing forth a river.[68] The Renaissance understood the achievements of the ancients through massive ruins and the massive hubris of such tales: to best those ancient splendors was a function of the "gran maniera."[69]

Nevertheless, evocation of those fabled

wonders betrayed a nostalgic longing to flee an imperfect present and to recapture a past the lofty grandeur of which colossal statuary conjured up in a particularly visceral way. In that sense, the colossus identified a temporal boundary, a gateway affording access to memory and to the enchanted realm of the historical imagination. As signpost, *genius loci*, repository of power, or source of magic, the colossus occupies, guards, and illuminates the frontier outposts of the spirit.

Midway between the skyscrapers of modern New York City and the green Long Island lawn from which the reader looks westward into the dim antiquity of the American heritage and the darkling plain of nature, F. Scott Fitzgerald interposes such a frontier place. It is a wasteland, called "the valley of ashes." A kind of no-man's-land relic of the war in Europe, it is a roadside purgatory of desolation, a parody on the wayside dinosaur park or miniature golf course, "a fantastic farm where ashes grow like wheat into ridges and hills and grotesque gardens, . . . where ashes take the forms of houses and chimneys and rising smoke."[70]

The ashes mingle the harsh, technological forms of Manhattan and the nurturing, pastoral forms of West Egg. The valley of ashes is a frontier of sorts, a dividing and hence a meeting point between East and West, city and country, past and future. Nick Carraway, the American pilgrim—heir of another Bunyan—must traverse this boundary at every juncture in his journey toward the self-realization that will reconcile him with his, with Gatsby's, and with America's stupendous dreams. The valley of ashes possesses one, single fixed landmark:

. . . above the gray land and the spasms of bleak dust which drift endlessly over it, you perceive, after a moment, the eyes of Doctor T. J. Eckleburg. The eyes of Doctor T. J. Eckleburg are blue and gigantic—their retinas are one yard high. They look out of no face, but, instead, from a pair of enormous yellow spectacles which pass over a non-existent nose. Evidently some wild wag of an oculist set them there to fatten his practice in the

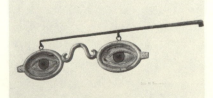

A shop sign with spectacles and big blue eyes, ca. 1875—the prototype for Fitzgerald's detailed description of Dr. Eckleburg's enormous eyes. Photo courtesy of the National Gallery of Art, Washington, D.C.; the Index of American Design.

borough of Queens, and then sank down himself into eternal blindness, or forgot them and moved away. But his eyes, dimmed a little by many paintless days under sun and rain, brood on over the solemn dumping ground.[71]

The colossal eyes of Dr. Eckleburg ask Nick and us to stop momentarily, just long enough to look at this psychic frontier and to understand the real-life motor trip across the valley of ashes as a metaphorical rite of passage. The eyes remind the reader of his physical and kinesthetic behavior. A direct glance from one pair of eyes into another produces the hiatus of forceful recognition and self-consciousness. The ordinary acts of looking at or through eyes direct attention toward the larger acts of apprehension and cognition. To say "I see" is to mean "I know." But the spectacles and the big blue eyes have been physically extrapolated from the human face and grotesquely enlarged: their scale is no longer human and familiar. Rather, the ensemble is superhuman, scaled to the place above which it hovers, in a frozen act of cosmic, unending appraisal.

Manipulation of scale was so basic to the crazes pursued with such manic determination by the sheiks and flappers of Gatsby's era that one small town mayor was moved to praise a young flagpole-sitter in the park for keeping "the old pioneer spirit of early America . . . alive today." Flagpole- and treetop-sitters, along with champion hot dog-, dill pickle-, raw egg- or clam-, and green pepper-eaters, stretched normal activities to disproportionate duration or indulged in them to the point of surfeit. They roosted too high in the sky, for far too long; they gobbled down far too much.[72] They behaved like greedy giants to stand out above the celebrity-mad mob.

The very last of the goofy fads of the 1920s was miniature golf, which, according to Frederick Lewis Allen, burst upon an unsuspecting America on September 3, 1929 — a month before the Great Crash — when Garnet Carter of Lookout Mountain, Tennessee, boarded a train for Miami to install the first roadside course.[73] In vain did Elmer Davis plump for the urban origins of the game, recalling links constructed atop a Manhattan skyscraper by John Ledbetter and his partner, Drake Delanoy, in 1926.[74] Miniature golf was the quintessential roadside attraction, a game of thwarted pastoral aspirations. Manuals on the subject, written for small businessmen who aimed to own courses, always stressed the importance of "prime suburban locations" adjacent to busy thoroughfares, of floodlights visible from the highway, of eye-catching billboards:

> Neon display signs announcing the fact that a miniature golf course is located here are very popular. Since the bulk of your play is night play, it seems rather advisable to have some sort of electric sign locating your course at night.[75]

Open land for courses was more readily available beyond the city limits. But the suburbs also were preferred because, as marketed by the promoters of patented putting surfaces and ball-return pipes, the game simulated country-club golf and the attendant folkways of country club members from the nation's West Eggs. And miniature golf improved on its prototype by eliminating snobbery, dues, and the need for suitable costumes. *The Nation* charted the descent of "the golf ball, formerly protected from *hoi polloi* by tight wrappings of exclusive country clubs and expensive paraphernalia," to the lower regions of society:

> [W]hen the pseudo-Klieg lights are playing full upon the humble householder from Hackensack, he may not only experience that comfortable country-club feeling superinduced by drooping plus fours and prehistoric posture; he may also be able to capture the illusion that he is John Barrymore at work.[76]

The whole "sporty" experience, with velvety greens made of crushed cottonseed hulls, cunning papier-mâché traps, and real water hazards—"fun exercise in the sunshine, which means health and happiness," pledged one ad—cost a mere 25 cents, a figure below which

"ALL RIGHT, GIRLS, COME IN, IT WON'T COST
YOU A CENT."

John Held, Jr.'s, conception of
"Al's Putt-Putt." From an illustration
by John Held, Jr., for *The Flesh Is
Weak* (1931).

operators were enjoined never to go, lest price
wars sully the swank reputation of the game.[77]

If F. Scott Fitzgerald wrote the script for the
20s, John Held, Jr., the leading cartoonist of
the day (and illustrator of Fitzgerald's *Tales of
the Jazz Age*) drew the pictures. His was the
amusing and stylish image of the "sheba" with
her short skirts, rolled stockings and bob, and
her button-nosed, brilliantined swains, in bags
and raccoon coats. Held also wrote and illustrated brittle short stories of his own, cynical
little vignettes of modern morals and foibles,
betraying a fine eye for textural detail. "The
Holy Bonds" followed the successful campaign
of Beulah, pregnant arch-flapper, to snare a
husband—any husband—in a tearing hurry.
Her appraising glance falls on Al, proprietor of
"Al's Putt-Putt," a young fellow "elegantly at-
tired in white linen golf knickerbockers with
blue cross-lines in the weave, a silk polo shirt,
short-sleeved and open at the throat. A skeleton
eye-shade was on his head."[78]

A poor man's parody of Bobby Jones, his
alarming ensemble is a form of advertising and,
in fact, Al aspires to the bright lights: he longs
to perform stunts, set endurance records, or
run a carnival. In the meantime, this former
owner of a roadside hot dog stand runs a "pee-
wee" golf course, laid out with his own hands
according to a set of plans printed in *Popular
Mechanics*.

Real sportsmen play by day, when ordinary
folks work. Al's "gayly lighted" course offered
a democratic sport for the working stiff, his
wife, and the kiddies, and no practice was
necessary:

It was the night life, and was giving the
two movie theaters keen competition.
The running electric signs of the theaters
were blinking to empty streets. The
course was crowded by those who felt the
need of inexpensive diversion. It was a
popular new fad, twenty-five cents a
game and an opportunity to make a small
bet. Those of the townspeople who were
not playing were standing around the
fence watching and making comments to
the players. A large, muslin banner an-

nounced "Al's Putt-Putt, twenty-five cents." The eighteen holes of the course occupied a vacant lot next to the gas-and-service station.[79]

By the time Held and the journalistic fraternity got around to analyzing the miniature golf phenomenon, the Depression was an established fact of life and fads seemed worse than silly. With tongue in cheek, *Harper's* opined that the miniature golf business might save the nation and restore prosperity if the frenzy to play continued.[80] The *Literary Digest* parodied tired presidential sermons on grassroots free enterprise in a report about a homemade "Wee-Willie" course in Flatbush, successfully operated by two little boys who charged their pals two pennies a round.[81] *Business Week* solemnly recited statistics on the vast quantities of concrete, lumber, empty lots, lightbulbs, and agricultural by-products absorbed in the construction of 25,000 new courses.[82] As the economy subsided into torpor, miniature golf was riding the crest of a $125,000,000 business boomlet.[83]

The wild popularity of the game variously known as Tom Thumb, Baby Grand, Pee-Wee, or Midget Golf is only partially explained by the low cost of playing and by the proliferation of patented courses that could be bought, complete in every detail, for as little as $4,500. The intrinsic appeal of the game is best understood by reviewing its genesis on the grounds of the Fairyland Inn, near Chattanooga. Around 1925 Garnet Carter, the hotelkeeper, built and heavily promoted a miniature "fairyland" for the children of his guests. In the woods adjacent to the resort, he contrived tiny caves and pools, and "scattered about in the most unexpected places were Little Red Riding Hood, Tom, Tom, the Piper's Son, Little Miss Muffet, the Ginger Bread Man, and others of the 'little people' so dear to the heart of childhood."[84] In 1926 Carter decided to add a little putting green, a junior version of the regulation model, to give the kids something to do in those nursery rhyme settings. The dwarf theme of "fairyland" prompted him to build a tiny, nine-hole golf course instead, and the children were ecstatic. The only problem was the parents:

Little girls posing at a miniature bridge on a California course, ca. 1930. From a plate in *Miniature Golf, A Treatise on the Subject* (1930).

"Papas and Mamas crowded the children off." Armed with a shrewd hunch that all grownups might be similarly affected, Carter put the first duplicate of his course on the market in 1929, and the great miniature golf fad began in earnest.[85]

In a "fairyland" full of storybook statues and toy-sized waterfalls, children enjoyed an advantage real life denied them: they were the absolute masters of their environment. Suddenly, magically, they were large enough to wander among caves and streams that, at normal scale, were menaces to the young. Suddenly, their physical skills were adequate to the demands of a game that, at normal scale, was too hard for kids. They were bigger and more consequential than the dwarf inhabitants of this realm; in the kingdom of the tiny, the child was a make-believe adult, or a giant from the storybooks. The effect of miniature golf on adults was comparable, and helps to explain the mass appeal of a fad the Depression ought to have nipped in the bud.

All the crazes of the 1920s made participants feel larger-than-life, a metaphor that became a reality on the premises of countless roadside Putt-Putts, where the world-famous Singer Midgets made special, live appearances as crowd-pleasing "touring pros." But miniaturization enlarged the self-esteem and enhanced the well-being of players in highly distinctive ways, understood by managers and golfers alike. One eyewitness, reporting from the Florida links in 1930, described good-natured banter between those on the fairways and their friends along the fences. The cry of "Hey, where's your plus-fours?" acknowledged that the admission fee bought a ticket to a fantasy of wealth and status, as well as a friendly diversion. The muslin banners along the highway were a frontier between a somber world of hard times and getting by, and a fantasyland of swaggering panache, a place where the player literally called the shots.[86]

Many of the celebrated courses of the period looked nothing at all like conventional golf courses. The so-called "novelty courses" were bedecked with hazards in the shape of London Bridge, little Dutch windmills, water wheels, lighthouses, cathedrals, or even skyscrapers from which balls were mysteriously expelled into distant traps. "The Chiquita" in South Pasadena, California, was a prime specimen of the genre:

> Its motif is The Covered Wagon. On Hole No. 2, which is Par 3, one shoots through a tiny covered wagon to a "hook" hole 25 feet away. On another fairway, real antelope hoofs and forelegs, stuck upright, furnish the hazard. Another is the half of a massive old wagon wheel which stands upright in the earth, so that the ball passes through the hub. Still another is the "water" hole, a grim desert scene with bleached bones scattered all about.[87]

Another "covered wagon" course in Los Angeles had a tame bear tethered to a little Conestoga parked near a tee; the bear was trained to snatch golfballs but could be bribed with chewing gum and candy bars.[88] A third course, in Pasadena proper, featured more exotic decor. One dogleg sent the ball toward "a Zulu hut, . . . thence through the Hut 28 feet to hole."[89]

The tiny buildings on miniature golf courses are colossi of sorts. Judged against the dimensions of the links, a little Cape Cod lighthouse straddling a diminutive fairway seems comparable to the size of the Pharos at Alexandria or the Colossus of Rhodes, the monster lighthouses of antiquity. What is out of scale in the ensemble is the player, who looms, Gulliverwise, over that setting. The golfer, paradoxically, is a colossus, too, larger by far than the colossal landmarks that trace his route through the links. And these architectural snippets are landmarks in both the literal and the figurative senses: they distinguish one little hole from the next, but they also replicate, in stunted versions, buildings that serve as place markers in the everyday world.

A wagon-train course in California with a live hazard. Note the rustic bridge in the background. From a plate in *Miniature Golf, A Treatise on the Subject* (1930).

THE GREAT AMERICAN ROADSIDE
Tourist Sculpture in Minnesota

Lighthouses, skyscrapers, and steeples are landmarks by virtue of their height and are often so designed. The Eiffel Tower, the Cape Cod lighthouse, the Dutch windmill, and the other stock accouterments of miniature golf courses are associated with special parts of the world and thus become landmarks in a global context. Strictly speaking, a building is not a colossus if it is not also a statue. Yet a dwarf replica of a Dutch windmill might give Pliny pause; insofar as the little structure is a three-dimensional representation of a prototype (and is designed as it is primarily *to* represent that prototype), it is a statue that, like other pieces of sculpture, conveys meaning. The Putt-Putt windmill, or skyscraper, or Eiffel Tower can tell stories of trips to fabulous, faraway places. The Zulu hut in Pasadena signifies "the dark continent": a swing around the course is an exotic jungle trek in the footsteps of Tarzan.

Standing by the side of an ordinary American highway, native huts, poking their tousled brows above illuminated banners, presented an odd enough spectacle to warrant a second glance, or perhaps a stop, even in California, where domestic architecture of the 1920s and 30s followed a similar bent. In 1939, novelist Nathaniel West took the reader on an armchair tour of the roadside architecture in one Los Angeles suburb:

Only dynamite would be of any use against the Mexican ranch houses, Samoan huts, Mediterranean villas, Egyptian and Japanese temples, Swiss chalets, Tudor cottages, and every possible combination of these styles that lined the slopes of the canyon.
When he noticed that they were all of plaster, lath and paper, he was charitable

and blamed their shape on the materials used. Steel, stone and brick curb a builder's fancy a little, forcing him to distribute his stresses and weights and to keep his corners plumb, but plaster and paper know no law, not even that of gravity.

On the corner of La Huerta Road was a miniature Rhine castle with tarpaper turrets pierced for archers. Next to it was a little highly colored shack with domes and minarets out of the *Arabian Nights.* Again he was charitable. Both houses were comic, but he didn't laugh. Their desire to startle was so eager and guileless.[90]

The Zulu huts of Pasadena were startling, and earnestly comical, in the cause of bigger gate receipts. Like the tract houses of *The Day of the Locust,* the windmills and steeples were less works of architecture than pictures of buildings — images of places, times, and dreams. The defunct antelope sticking up out of the ground at a "covered wagon" golf course finds a precise counterpart in the "life-size, realistic reproduction" of a dead horse West puts in the bottom of a swimming pool, during a movie-colony party. "Its legs stuck up stiff and straight," it was expensive, and according to the hostess, existed solely "to amuse." "Isn't it marvelous!" she exclaims, "jumping up and down excitedly like a little girl."[91]

The marvel is the sheer incongruousness of the dead horse in the mogul's pool, although West implies that the act of putting it there is also a marvel, of a different and a more sinister order. [92] The freakishness of the gesture and the image taps an ancient vein of American humor, however, and from that same source — the grotesque disproportion of the tall tale — comes the seriocomedy of miniature golf on "novelty" links. To the floodlit oasis by the side of the road come sober adults, bent on laughter and humor and play. There, by giddy turns, the players are idle millionaires, and mighty giants, and little girls and boys caught up in stirring, patently bogus adventures in the fastness of Africa and the capitals of Europe. Or,

This modern-day course on Como Avenue, in Saint Paul, Minnesota, produces a surreal effect by using colossi as hazards. Many of the same fiberglass animals appear elsewhere in the state as civic monuments. Photo by Bruce White.

Children adapt readily to the make-believe demands of colossal statuary. Photo by Bruce White.

with a dead antelope and a live bear as props, they follow the wagon trails of the Wild West back into the saga of history.

Miniature golf is a creature of the highway, the flivver, the suburb, and America's westering itch for perpetual mobility. It is altogether fitting, therefore, that the decor of this roadside attraction should simulate a tourist's-eye-view of travels in the wide, wide world. The roadside colossi at the local Putt-Putt guard the frontier of reality, and the highway that carries the motorist to "The Chiquita" winds, by imperceptible degrees, off the American roadmap, into a world of wishes and dreams. To the tourist, travel is a release from routine and from everyday constraints. All things are possible on the roadside, a privileged zone, strewn with marvels for the delectation of the wayfarer.

In the 1920s, the American highway came to resemble the fantastic landscape of a dream so closely that it was hardly necessary to drive any distance at all to inspect half the wonders of the known world. Consider, for example, this burlesque travelogue by Sinclair Lewis, describing a drive down a freshly paved, midwestern route:

Say, that day was a revelation of progress. When I first drove that road, it was just a plain dirt road running through a lot of unkempt farms, and now every mile or so you'd find a dandy up-to-date hot-dog stand—some like little log-cabins and some like Chinese pagodas or Indian wigwams or little small imitations of Mount Vernon about ten feet high, and all like that, and stocking every known refreshment for the inner man—hot dogs and apple pie and chewing-gum and cigars and so forth—and of course up-to-date billboards all along the road to diversify it.[93]

George Babbitt is the audience for this soliloquy, delivered by his pal Lowell Schmaltz, *The Man Who Knew Coolidge* of Lewis's 1928 novella. The Babbitts are planning a vacation trip and Schmaltz has promised to help by hitting the high points of his epic drive from Minnesota to Yellowstone. Only after 20 pages of breathless narrative do Babbitt and the reader begin to realize the awful truth: Schmaltz and his "missus" got barely two days west of home! But, after the wigwams and pagodas, after tiny Mount Vernons and pioneer cabins, what could Yellowstone have offered to match the panoply of enchantments lining U.S. 10, all the way from "Zenith" to Billings, via the Black Hills?

Six years after Lowell Schmaltz started off for Yellowstone, but—thanks to architectural surprises en route—detoured to old Virginny, Chinatown, and the Old West, *Fortune* mounted an investigative report on "The Great American Roadside." It was a lavish affair, with original illustrations by John Steuart Curry, one of the Midwestern Regionalist painters. And it owed its inspiration to Lowell Schmaltz and the roadside garden of midwestern delights "square in the middle of Mr. Sinclair Lewis' mythical state of Winnemac." The study focused on the economics of "an American Institution . . . founded upon a solid rock: the restlessness of the American people." The Depression, the editors opined, had done little to keep tourists off the 900,000 miles of new, hard-surfaced highway laid down since the first Fords went "a-gipsying."[94] Perhaps prices had fallen a bit at "these curious little broods of frame and log and adobe shacks which dot the roadside with their Mother Goose and their Chic Sale architecture." But inside, the shelves were still stocked with the curiosities that their curious shapes existed to advertise—curiosities in untold numbers. Why, even a veteran buyer for Woolworth's might quail at the prospect of working the miniature Mount Vernons of U.S. 10:

> For the restless taste of a restless people would run him ragged keeping up with the demand for such staples of American *turismo* as rag and rubber animals, little jig-sawed animals to set up on the lawn, sponge rock for the rock garden, slips of boxwood from Virginia estates, carved coconuts, birch-bark canoes, windmills,

This ice cream stand in Berlin, Connecticut, was illustrated in the *Fortune* article. Photo courtesy of the Library of Congress.

fox tails for the radiator cap, redwood bark, snake-skin belts, ash trays made of shell, pennants, baby alligators, little crates of kumquats, Civil War bullets (minnie balls), stalactites, balsam cushions, and turtles carved with the name of the young blade's girl. And the complete merchant would also be in the antique business and the native-pottery trade and run a thousand local textile industries as well. [95]

The gimcracks were touted by a cacophonous chorus of billboards, and beneath the signs, the log cabins and the tepees increased and multiplied and swelled in the sun, growing more bizarre with every passing season. Lowell Schmaltz had once marveled at a miniature Mount Vernon. From Connecticut to California, *Fortune* found stranger sights at every turn in the highway—"stands built like tamales, tea rooms built like teapots, papier-mâché owls lettered 'I-SCREAM', laughing swine with Neon teeth (again a tamale stand), and in fact almost any eye-widening outlandishness you can imagine!"[96] Out there on "The Great American Roadside," *Fortune* found the roadside colossus.

The colossal eyes of Doctor T. J. Eckleburg are, of course, a roadside colossus, a symbolic advertising device as old as Rome and a reminder that three-dimensional shop signs, such as the wooden cigarstore Indians of the 18th and 19th centuries, are the distant ancestors of the giant burgerboys and happy chefs and chickens and ice cream cones of the American highway today.[97] The primal Paul Bunyan of 1930s Minnesota, and his kin—along with the newer hyperbolic fowl in Rothsay, Vergas, Pelican Rapids, Virginia, and Wheaton, Minnesota; the fish in Nevis, Baudette, Ray, Erskine, Bena, and Garrison; the sea-serpent in Crosby; the otter in Fergus Falls; the Holstein cow in Bongards; the deer in Deerwood and Starbuck; the Dala horse in Mora; Smokey the Bear in International Falls; the giant ear of corn in Olivia; the Jolly Green Giant in Blue Earth; "Big Ole, the Viking" in Alexandria; St. Urho in Menahga; an early and exceedingly

A roadside ice-cream cone, near Wadena, Minnesota. Photo by Liz Harrison.

These jolly characters are scattered across the region. Photo by the author.

The Long Lake Loon, in Vergas, Minnesota. Photo by Liz Harrison.

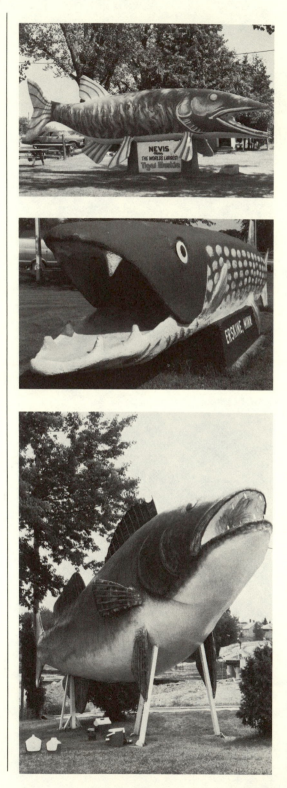

The "World's Largest Tiger Muskie" in Nevis. Photo by Liz Harrison.

A Northern in Erskine's lakefront park. Photo by Liz Harrison.

Another big fish—"Willie the Walleye" in Baudette, on the Rainy River. Photo by Liz Harrison.

The Big Fish Supper Club in Bena. Photo by Liz Harrison.

Smokey and his cubs, at International Falls. Photo by Liz Harrison.

The sign on the door reads, "Do not damage the teeth!" Photo by Liz Harrison.

"Big Ole," the Viking, stands in the middle of a highway in Alexandria. Photo by the author.

Garrison's Walleye, erected by the
local Commercial Club, is mobile: it
can also serve as a parade float.
Photo by Liz Harrison.

The sea serpent on the shore of
Serpent Lake in Crosby, Minnesota.
Such a creature also figures in some
versions of the Paul Bunyan myth.
Photo by Liz Harrison.

A similar fish graced the Polk
County, Wisconsin, float in the 1983
Wannigan Days festival parade in
Taylor's Falls, Minnesota. Photo by
Bruce White.

Colossi—in this case, Pillsbury's
corporate Doughboy—also appear in
the Saint Paul Winter Carnival
Parade. Photo by Bruce White.

A feature of the daily parade at the Minnesota State Fair is this colossal fiberglass bull, attended by large, humanoid eggs. Photo by Bruce White.

The cow in Bongards, Minnesota. Photo by the author.

What seems to be a parade float is actually a trick photograph, a journalistic hoax printed as an April Fool joke: "The Largest Fish Ever Caught." *Honolulu Star-Bulletin.*

"Lucy," a giant cow who ate pine trees and gave liniment instead of milk, was one of Paul Bunyan's companions in the Red River storybooks. From an illustration by W. B. Laughead.

The giant pelican in Pelican Rapids. Photo by Liz Harrison.

Not, strictly speaking, a colossus, the sculptural symbol for the town of Starbuck, Minnesota, was made from an electric Christmas star welded to a lawn ornament. Photo by the author.

Duplicates of the leaping stag in Deerwood, Minnesota, are found on several miniature golf courses and at the entrance to "Deertown," near Park Rapids. Photo by the author.

St. Urho chased the grasshoppers out of Finland, and is the Scandinavian answer to St. Patrick. A bronze plaque at his feet describes rituals celebrated in his honor in Menahga, Minnesota. Photo by Liz Harrison.

This 32-foot statue of Hermann the Cheruscan, atop its elaborate pedestal in New Ulm, Minnesota, was erected by German immigrants. In intent and technique, the statue resembles *Liberty* in New York Harbor. Hermann was made of copper sheeting hung on a metal skeleton constructed by the Milwaukee Bridge and Iron Works in 1890. Photo courtesy of New Ulm Area Chamber of Commerce.

Chief Wenonga guards Battle Lake,
Minnesota. Photo by Liz Harrison.

Chief Mon-Si-Moh ("Moose Dung")
at Thief River Falls, Minnesota.
Photo by Liz Harrison.

The Cloquet Voyageur. Photo by Liz Harrison.

"Pierre, the Voyageur," near Two Harbors, Minnesota, rolls his eyes and turns his head. Photo by Liz Harrison.

Madison, Minnesota's new cod, a
week after its ceremonial installation.
Photo by the author.

serious "Hermann the German" in New Ulm;
and a clutch of voyageurs and Indians scattered
across the state from Thief River Falls to Crane
Lake—are signs.[98]

Whether patented corporate trademarks in
the round or localized, cottage-industry em-
blems fabricated to convey a sense of a town's
unique claim to recognition, these colossi
function like advertisements on several levels.
They point, in more or less specific ways, to
commodities for sale: chicken sandwiches,
hunting and fishing spots, local industries, a
corporate enclave, a Barnumlike, roadside
curiosity of history. Or they point to catchy
slogans that, in turn, point toward the local
Rexall and the Hardware Hank. Thus it came
about that in the high, steamy summer of 1983,
the Chamber of Commerce of Madison, Minnesota, erected a 25-foot fiberglass codfish on
the edge of town. Madison's elders understood
the cash value of colossi:

> As far as we know, this is the biggest cod-
> fish in America. It's just as big as the
> Jolly Green Giant that sticks up over the
> freeway outside of Le Sueur [sic], only
> we're horizontal. It's not only big but
> portable. This is a codfish that deserves
> an audience, so we're making it adaptable
> to parades. You've got a parade, we'll
> come with the codfish.[99]

Now Madison, Minnesota, has neither lakes
nor fishes, but it does have plenty of Scandi-
navians, who turn out en masse for an annual
banquet of "lutefisk," an ethnic delicacy com-
posed of cod. On that slender warrant, Madison proclaimed itself "The Lutefisk Capital of
the U.S.A." and proposed to use the big pink
and green codfish rising above the prairie on
Highway 75 to draw the tourists of America to
western Minnesota. According to the owner of
the Madison Super Valu, the prime mover in
the campaign to raise the $8,000 cost of making
the fish and hauling it in from Sparta, Wisconsin, the effort was long overdue:

> The problem we've got with attracting
> more tourists than we do is that when

you look at a map, Madison doesn't leap
out at you. We don't have any rivers in
town or any mountains. We've got a very
aggressive business community here and
a really lovely place, but Hwy. 212 goes
just south of here. Hwy. 75 is a straight
shot from Iowa to Canada, and we want
to slow some of these people down. We
don't think you can very well ignore a
25-foot codfish.[100]

By that logic, an 11½-foot eagle was almost
as hard to overlook, and a month later, Remer,
Minnesota, put one up right beside Tony
Thurmes's OK Hardware:

> This whole thing started when the Re-
> mer Civic Club decided to put some signs
> up on Hwy. 200. Somebody said, "Why
> not a statue, too?"
> After rejecting logging as a theme be-
> cause it had been overdone and wild rice
> because it would be hard to work into a
> statue, the eagle was chosen.[101]

The Remer eagle was also new in the
summer of 1983. Photo by Liz
Harrison.

Remer declared itself "The Eagle Capital of the
World" and sold enough raffle tickets (in a
town of 396 souls) to put up the big bird and
to hand out some cash prizes at a gala dedication ceremony, replete with bands, beauty
queens, speeches, and a softball game. Then,
according to a reliable witness, the celebrants
"drifted across the street to the Eagle's Eye Inn
or up to the municipal liquor store and bar for
ice cream and other restoratives. . . . "[102]

Rothsay became "The Prairie Chicken
Capital of Minnesota" almost by accident. A
guest speaker at a meeting of the Agassiz Study
Club just happened to mention that the bird
was native to the area. The members mulled it
over and, in the spring of 1975, asked the
Rothsay Commercial Club to take up the possi-
bility of designating their town the official
capital. In towns of 448, organizational direc-
torates tend to overlap. What the Agassiz Study
Club asked, the Commercial Club granted with
alacrity. Art Fosse, a civic-minded citizen,
"offered the use of his shop and equipment to
assist in constructing an appropriate monu-

The Rothsay prairie chicken. Note concrete walkways around the statue. In the summer, the town puts a picnic table here, and corn grows right up to the roadside park. Photo by Marion Nelson.

ment," researched the appearance of the species at the University of Minnesota, and became a folk sculptor, overnight:

> Pipes and other pieces of steel were bent and restructured to form a profile and this, in turn, was welded into a subframe and base assembly. . . . After a protective covering was put on the metal surfaces . . . and wire mesh was put in place, the form was ready for cement work and plastering. Many area farmers donated time and effort into the cement-packing effort, Fosse noted. Two high school students . . . came to Fosse's shop to assist with welding. . . . Professional artist Dale Western, a Rothsay native, utilized his expertise and skills to provide an exquisite finishing touch and the monument was ready to make a public entrance.[103]

The big bird was unveiled on June 15, 1976, in a ceremony that kicked off local observances of the nation's Bicentennial. It was a nasty day, with a cold wind, but the weather did not faze radio and television crews from as far away as Fargo and Fergus Falls. The debut of the monument even rated a front-page picture in the *Minneapolis Tribune*, which noted, in a caption, that Rothsay stood in "the heart of the narrow midwestern prairie-chicken range" but admitted to no puzzlement over how the natives reconciled a 9,000-pound replica of a male specimen, doing "its colorful mating dance," with America's 200th birthday.[104] The publicity value of roadside curiosities, it would seem, increases in direct proportion to their curiousness.

Minnesota's propensity for littering the highways with fiberglass fauna has not been without its critics, however. A 1978 editorial in the *Mankato Free Press* took a jaundiced view of Blue Earth's upcoming dedication of the $45,000 Green Giant, and of other such costly effusions of civic pride. Mankato, it should be noted, had no colossus. Thus its spokesperson was free to charge overzealous Chambers of Commerce elsewhere with opening a nasty "Pandora's box of statuary advertising regional attractions." The editor conjured up terrible visions of aesthetic blight along the interstate. At the Rochester interchange, a 45-foot stethoscope to tout the Mayo Clinic! At Worthington, a "gargantuan gobbler" to advertise the annual Turkey Days! And so it went:

> At I-90 and Hwy. 13, there could be two statues: one of a gigantic bullhead (for Waterville's ego) and one of an immense kolacky (for Montgomery's ego). I-90, in Minnesota, at least, would pretty soon get a reputation for being visually tacky, however. But if that's what the state's residents want, that's what they'll deserve getting.[105]

Waterville celebrates Bullhead Days every June. Every September, Montgomery holds Kolacky Days, and, along the parade route or during the big softball tournament, serves 2,000 dozen of those wonderful Bohemian buns with the poppy-seed filling.[106] There is, alas, no giant pastry in Montgomery, and there is, as yet, no monstrous bullhead in Waterville. But the *Free Press* satire, despite its disparaging tone, does underscore the relationship between colossi and the town festivals that play a major role in the economic and cultural life of Minnesota. The Paul Bunyan statues in Bemidji were created expressly to promote a winter carnival, and since the 1930s the number of similar annual celebrations has increased dramatically. The 1983 register of summertime festivals listed more than 300 such occasions, ranging from ordinary county fairs, to Paul Bunyan Days at his cradleside in Akeley, to the Lindbergh Air Fair in Little Falls.[107]

Although local details vary, the basic format of the town gala is not dissimilar to the program for the 11th Annual Swedish Festival, held in Cambridge in June of 1983. Cambridge mounted a half-marathon, a canoe race, a golf match, a softball tournament, special church services, a pancake brunch, and a chicken barbecue. There was a Miss Cambridge Pageant and there was a big Cattlemen's Show. But the vast majority of features were designed to bring people into downtown Cambridge, where

The Dala Horse in Mora—a replica of the Dalecarlian horses carved in Mora, Sweden, since the 1840s—is a reminder of the town's Scandinavian heritage. It was built by the local Jaycees in 1971 as a tourist attraction; ever since, Mora has billed itself "Home of the World's Largest Dala Horse." Photo by Liz Harrison.

Minnesota's only floating colossus, the Virginia loon. Photo by Liz Harrison.

special Jaycee activities and a window display contest highlighted the retail promotion that was one important reason for launching an Annual Swedish Festival in the first place. Another, to be sure, was the feeling of community—of cultural solidarity—fostered by the planning process itself and by an 8-day schedule of events, all of which involved large groups of children, or adults, or both, coming together for the manure spreader race, the parade, or a visit from the Paul Bunyan Storyteller of Long Lake, who offered an hour of "tall tales" at the East Central Regional Library.[108]

On the second afternoon of the Swedish Festival, the people of Cambridge were invited to Riverside Park, where Art Moe, a self-styled "Chainsaw Artist" from Stone Lake, Wisconsin, was slated to "carve a Scandivanian mythological figure." The statue made during the demonstration was not an outsize monument, nor was it calculated to attract tourists to Cambridge to see something so unique as to justify the detour. Indeed, despite feeble efforts to make the world at large beat a path to downtown Cambridge every June, the Swedish Festival remains a local or, at best, a county event.[109] Towns with colossi conduct their festive affairs somewhat differently. Bemidji's Paul Bunyan Water Carnival, Brainerd's Paul Bunyan Festival, Virginia's Land of the Loon Festival, Crane Lake's Voyageur Days, Mora's Dala Days, Muskie Days in Nevis, and Corn Capital Days in Olivia cast a wider net into the stream of tourism. Roadside colossi advertise town festivals and, in turn, become the foci of such attention as festivals draw to the existence, the charms, and the commercial advantages of their host communities.

A 20-foot, locally produced, fiberglass loon floating in Silver Lake is the centerpiece of the Annual Land of the Loon Area Ethnic Arts and Crafts Festival, its logo, one of its early by-products, and its prime attraction: every June, the streets leading to the heart of Virginia and so to this unique, waterborne colossus, are festooned with banners bearing its likeness.[110] The Voyageur Days fete is harder to find, since Crane Lake is a bit off the beaten path. "You would never pass through it on the way to someplace else because that is where the road ends"; and without the colossus dominating the fork of St. Louis County Road 424, where an even smaller lane veers toward town, Voyageur Days in the tiny resort community might be a most exclusive affair. But in the early 1960s, the local Commercial Club had the monument made down in Minneapolis, and began initiating "pork eaters" (a.k.a., tourists) in a series of arcane rites of portage that culminate in the award of a tasseled cap, a sash, and a souvenir certificate of membership in the fraternity of woodland heroes:

The Crane Lake Voyageur. Photo by Liz Harrison.

> Crane Lake people have adopted the Voyageur as their patron saint and have erected a colorful 13½-foot statue of him. They claim he symbolizes Minnesota far better than the lowly gopher, and with no apologies to the Bemidji and Brainerd areas they contend he is more picturesque than Paul Bunyan and the blue ox. "Why adopt a mythical monster," they say, "when we have a 200 year history of these very real miniature giants known as the French Voyageurs?"[111]

Although colossi advertise festivals, statuary and organized revelry are complementary assertions of local identity. They mark off a stretch of time and a node of place from the continuum of the summertime highway. Colossi locate the edge of town, the route to the business district, its principal attractions. Once over the borderline between movement and stasis, the tourist has effectively left ordinary circumstances behind and is ready for the games, the beauty queens, the costumes, the rituals, and the comestibles with which Americans observe festive occasions.

So it happened that pop singer Olivia Newton-John demanded only "fresh bread and two dozen ears of corn" for her services as grand marshall of the Olivia, Minnesota, Centennial Parade in which she appeared, wearing a 10-gallon hat, jeans, and a western shirt, astride a horse.[112] The 1978 campaign to "Bring Olivia to Olivia" brought a publicity

A giant ear of corn perched atop a picnic shelter in Olivia, Minnesota. Photo by the author.

Note the mottoes, the 4-H trash barrels, and the edge of a picnic table. Photo by the author.

bonanza to a community of 3,200 already determined to be noticed for something. For years, corn festivals of one sort and another—the titles and the programs varied—had been organized around the annual "corn feed" in Henton Park.[113] By the time of the Centennial, however, Olivia had become "The Corn Capital" of the civilized world, and the home of "Corn Capital Days."

That declaration of importance is rendered permanent, tactile, and somewhat alarming by the colossal ear of golden corn that stands atop a picnic shelter on the outskirts of Olivia. The Crane Lake Voyageur is startling, too, as it pops out of 20 miles of featureless woods. The Virginia loon begs for a double take, punctuated by the squeal of brakes. Olivia's vegetal beacon in the sky jolts the passerby with the message that here—right here—begins an exceptional, nay extraordinary town, altogether different from the rest of the little burgs strung out like so many beads along Highway 212 from Glencoe to Granite Falls. The Olivia colossus recognizes and honors the urge to come to a shuddering halt at the base of this tall tale cast in fiberglass. The town has provided picnic tables, a drinking fountain, a charcoal grill, a parking area paved with gravel, a couple of trash barrels, and a fiberglass port-a-potty on the site.[114]

The gesture is hospitable, an anticipation of the party manners adopted every July for Corn Capital Days. But even without a festival in progress, the wayside park invites the motorist to mimic the leisured rituals of festival times, and to concentrate on enjoyment in a pastoral setting, improved with every urban amenity. In Rothsay, the volunteers who made the concrete prairie chicken were pleased when the area adjacent to the monument became "a roadside park complete with sidewalks, trees," and the mandatory picnic bench.[115] In fact, such roadside rest stops invariably accompany Minnesota colossi, even when the scrap of land from which the statue rises is scarcely bigger than the requisite picnic table.[116]

The little park laid out around the statue of the mallard in Wheaton, Minnesota, is especially elaborate. The duck itself sits in a little lakelike basin made of concrete and labeled, "Traverse," "Land of Ducks." Then come rows of plantings. And next are the green concrete letters inset in the sidewalk that circles the colossus. The text spells out the finer points of Traverse County: "Hunting," "Farming," "Living," and "Fishing." The picnic table is flanked by trash containers hand-painted by the 4-H, and bearing other hortatory slogans. At night, a spotlight illuminates the whole tidy montage. By day or by night, the 26-foot duck in its picture-perfect park issues an unforgettable, almost irresistible invitation to dally in Wheaton. Robert Bruns, the Fergus Falls teacher who is the father of the mallard and several other homemade colossi in western Minnesota, had just that effect in mind in 1959 when he persuaded Wheaton to spend $1,200 on the project:

The Wheaton mallard, made by Robert Bruns of Fergus Falls, Minnesota. Photo by the author.

> "Wheaton is proud of its ducks on Lake Traverse so I promoted the building of the duck to honor them," Bruns said. "I designed it from a paperweight duck, a Grain Belt Beer ad and a dime-store statue. . . . [P]eople maybe won't remember Wheaton, Minn., but they'll remember, 'Oh, yeah, that's where we saw the duck!' "[117]

Bob Bruns's otter in Fergus Falls. Photo by Liz Harrison.

That the lineage of the Wheaton mallard should have included a beer ad is hardly surprising. The roadside colossus is an advertisement and, like all ads, its function is to capture attention and linger in memory. Hence, the strange case of Big Vic, the protest colossus, a 25-foot-tall, 2,300-pound fiberglass portrait of Vic Davis wearing a voyageur's outfit and carrying a big musket. The statue was made in Sparta, Wisconsin, flown by helicopter to an island in Voyageurs National Park, and firmly bolted to a 24,000-pound concrete pedestal on the shoreline by Mr. Davis to draw attention to certain baleful federal land acquisition practices. Davis objected to Park Service policies restricting the development of private lands within the park. One lone resident, however strong his convictions, was easier to intimidate than many; so, in the spring of 1980, Davis

Vic Davis with "Big Vic," the protest colossus. Photo courtesy of *Minneapolis Star and Tribune*.

began selling off square-foot parcels of his island in Rainy Lake at $19.95 apiece, reasoning that if Uncle Sam had to deal with thousands of owners, the proceedings would be held up indefinitely. Big Vic was an advertisement for the scheme and Davis was reported "confident the statue will spur more sales:"

> "If they want the park . . . they're going to have to pay for it. The statue is a symbol and warning to politicians and bureaucrats in Washington, D.C., that everything is going to court from now on." Davis plans to install a couple of picnic tables and barbecue stands on the island to further demonstrate his defiance of park service policy. . . . [118]

The government struck back by levying customs fines against the hapless helicopter pilot who had strayed across an international border while ferrying Big Vic to his mooring.[119] Finally, federal agents seized the island, statue, picnic tables, and all. In May of 1982, Vic Davis responded with a second statue, a 3,100-pound self-portrait almost identical to the first, but erected within sight of the proposed visitors' center for Voyageurs Park.[120] Although the U.S. District Court later ruled that the government owed Davis more than $90,000 for his island, the litigation and the proliferation of giant, defiant voyageurs promised to continue.[121] Nothing draws a crowd quicker than a big statue.

That much was clear to Jim Lelm of Harvey, North Dakota, when he bought Og, "the largest mechanical ape in these parts—and perhaps in any part" in 1982. Og's checkered career began in an amusement park in Dickinson, North Dakota; in 1978, he migrated to "Rawhide City," a tourist attraction in Mandan that promptly went belly up, leaving the ape in a sorry state of disrepair. His teeth were chipped and his pelt had been pockmarked by voracious woodpeckers. Lelm hauled the remains to Harvey on a flatbed truck and aimed to anchor Og to the roof of his farm implement store, with his eyes rolling and his jaws clenching once again. When questioned about the propriety of doing business beneath the sign of a 2-ton, 30-foot-tall, 45-foot-wide, animated gorilla, Mr. Lelm invoked the civic precedents of Jamestown, home of "The World's Largest Buffalo," and New Salem, home of "The World's Biggest Cow":

> Because other towns display such things as large buffaloes or cows for attention, Lelm believes Og is OK for Harvey, which has a population of about 2,600. "If we paint him and fix him up, I can't see where it will hurt. Anything to draw people into town is good for everybody," Lelm said. . . . [H]e's counting on Og's presence to be associated with his business. "If you can't remember the address, a person can always remember that it's the place with the big ape on the roof. I think the town will gain by it. There's not many towns in North Dakota that have a 30-foot-high ape."[122]

But there are towns elsewhere in the Midwest with statues titled in superlatives. Had chauvinism not induced a certain myopia in the matter of colossi, Mr. Lelm might also have cited "The World's Largest Pheasant," at the Plains Motel in Huron, South Dakota, or "Albert, the World's Largest Bull," in Audubon, Iowa, or "The Giant Walk-Thru Musky (½-city-block long and 5 stories tall)"—clearly the world's largest of its kind—at the National Freshwater Fishing Hall of Fame in Hayward, Wisconsin.[123] Like "The World's Largest Ball of Twine" saved up and exhibited by Francis Johnson of Darwin, Minnesota, or the facsimile of "The Largest Cheese in the History of Mankind" stowed in the trailer of a semi parked in Neillsville, Wisconsin, these statues claim absolute hegemony in size in order to increase their value as roadside curiosities, destined for a mention in Ripley's "Believe It or Not" column and for full-color reproduction on a postcard.[124]

"Salem Sue," in New Salem, North Dakota. Russ Hanson photograph, courtesy of North Dakota Tourism Promotion.

The "Walk-Thru" fish at the National Freshwater Fishing Hall of Fame, Hayward, Wisconsin. Photo by Bruce White.

"Chatty Belle" stands alongside "The Largest Cheese in the History of Mankind" in Neillsville, Wisconsin. From a McGrew (Kansas City, Missouri) postcard.

POSTCARDS, SOUVENIRS, AND COME-ONS
Wayside Giants Sell the American Dream

Such cartoon postcards are sold in both Brainerd and Bemidji, Minnesota. From an NMN, Inc. (Crosslake, Minnesota) postcard.

On postcards, corn is also larger than life. From a Dunlap Post Card Co. (Omaha, Nebraska) postcard.

Unnaturally large objects were illustrated on the tall-tale postcards that enjoyed a national vogue in the decade before World War I. Throughout the 1920s and 30s, however, the Midwest remained the major client for and producer of such trick images.[125] A card made from pictures taken by a Chinook, Montana, photographer, for instance, shows a massive spud, entirely filling a Great Northern flatcar. A sign affixed to the cargo reads: "The Way We Raise Potatoes in North Dakota."[126] Similar pictorial greetings manufactured and sold in the Midwest today display an ear of Iowa corn larger than a tractor, a loaf of good Kansas bread as big as a wheatfield, a huge Minnesota walleye about to swamp a canoe, fisherman and all.[127] Occasionally, what seems to be a falsified montage is a genuine picture of something odd, as in the case of postcards showing a buxom young woman perched atop a saddle on the back of a 16-foot, leaping walleye ("The World's Largest") at Lake Kabetogama, near Ray, Minnesota. The concrete fish is really there, and a staircase permits access to its saddle.[128]

Bemused by receipt of a postcard mailed from Los Angeles, showing a truck-sized California watermelon, Paul Fussell devotes a lengthy digression in his recent study of British travel literature to the related issues of scale and wayside curiosities. The traveler's world, Fussell argues, is never quite like the ordinary one because "travel itself, even the most commonplace trip, is an implicit quest for anomaly." Tall-tale postcards commemorate encounters with the strange and the unfamiliar, albeit the oddities observed by Lowell Schmaltz on his abortive drive to Yellowstone are of a different order of magnitude from the

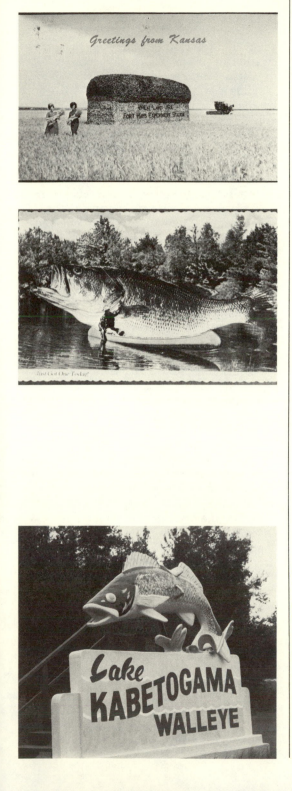

The caption on the reverse reads, "A field of wheat and a giant loaf of bread symbolize the role of Kansas as 'Wheatland, U.S.A.'" From a Dunlap Post Card Co. (Omaha, Nebraska) postcard.

This card is available in almost any resort town in the upper Midwest. From a Plastichrome (Boston, Massachusetts) postcard.

The saddle on the back of the colossal walleye near Ray, Minnesota (reached by a hidden ladder in the rear), allows amateur photographers to produce their own tall-tale postcards. Photo by Liz Harrison.

giant North Dakota potato. Nonetheless, the creation and dissemination of pictorial tall tales in postcard form testifies to the general understanding that tourists are lured to a given place by anomalies:

> Their function is to attract tourists by implying the anomalous fecundity of the area, most often California or the American Middle West. To this end, they depict bizarre hypertrophied vegetables or Brobdingnagian fruits reposing on large wagons and railway flat-cars; outsized birds and poultry, often so large as to threaten human life and the balance of nature; immense fish and rabbits large enough to be saddled and ridden; as well as anomalies harder to translate into an invitation to tourists, like monstrous grasshoppers, or chickens with the heads of pretty girls, or the "jackalope," a jackrabbit equipped with antlers, or fish with fur instead of scales. That these things are "photographed" adds to the comedy, parodying the more sober traveler's assumption that he may not be believed without bringing home photographic evidence.[129]

"Real" jackalopes were souvenirs before they were postcard subjects. Although "lopecards," overprinted with the name of the town in question, can be bought throughout the West and the Midwest, the genuine article was invented in Douglas, Wyoming, "The Jackalope Capital of the World," in 1934, by Ralph Herrick, a local taxidermist, and his brother Doug. The Herrick jackalope is a mythical beast, fleeter than the fastest antelope, and bigger than the largest jackrabbit. Tall tale becomes reality when the skeptic comes face to face with a creature consisting of deer antlers mounted on the head of a stuffed rabbit. Since the Herrick boys started making them, tourists have carried off 3,500 trophy jackalopes. Visitors may apply for jackalope "hunting permits" issued by the Chamber of Commerce. And they always take pictures of one another, posing alongside the 8-foot statue of the jackalope on Center Street.[130]

One North Dakota Spud

The Way we Raise Potatoes in North Dakota

GREAT NORTHERN 85155

A tall-tale "spud" postcard. From a Charles E. Morris (Chinook, Montana) postcard.

Colossi are advertisements that point to commodities for sale—resorts, or roadside curiosities, or, in the case of a big Paul Bunyan, an opportunity to escape from the gritty tedium of the highway into an amusing, diverting storybook legend. Apart from souvenir ashtrays, Paul Bunyan sells a momentary suspension of purposefulness. Whether in Bemidji or in Brainerd, the tall-tale hero reincarnated as "The Largest Lumberjack in the World" sells time—a break in the course of ordinary time— much as Eckleburg's eyes, deprived of their original commercial purpose, symbolize a rent in the tissue of reality, a portal beyond which the orgiastic future of the imagination and the verdant dreams of the American past still beckon and glimmer.

Whatever the service or commodity offered, the sign must first capture attention. In magazine ads of Gatsby's era, scale guaranteed memorability by administering a jolt of dislocation. The color layouts in the *Ladies' Home Journal* are, perhaps, a bit more lavish than

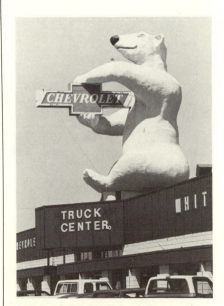

A famous commercial colossus marks an auto dealership in the suburbs of the Twin Cities. Photo by Bruce White.

Scale is clearly an issue in this advertisement. From *Ladies' Home Journal* (May, 1923).

The product dwarfs the customer. From *Ladies' Home Journal* (May, 1919).

Gum fills the field of vision. From *Ladies' Home Journal* (September, 1920).

most, but in composition they are altogether typical of the period. In a *Journal* offering of 1923, a Royal Baking Powder can is so big that a pastry chef can dance on its lid. A 1919 soap bar is as large as a laundry basket; a 1920 package of gum is as large as a harvester's fruit basket.[131] Monster products push forward in reverse perspective, zooming toward the consumer, impinging on her world with a force rendered doubly potent by the seemingly diminished scale of the everyday realities abandoned to shrivel in the pictorial background.

In the closed environment of a page, embedded in type, stoppage by scale is relatively easy to achieve. The same two-dimensional pictures, hung perpendicular to a row of shop facades, also operate effectively on the pedestrian concourse. But the automobile changed the character of signage decisively. In the early 1920s, long-distance driving was a nightmare of missed turns, frantic hunts for landmarks, and quarrels over whether the signpost at the last crossroads, bristling with hand-lettered directional arrows, had or had not been rotated by pranksters. The Federal Highway Act of 1921 mandated a uniform system of shapes and numbers for the markers on designated U.S. routes. By 1925, order had emerged from wayside chaos. It was possible for the tourist to rely on Uncle Sam's directions and the free map from the filling station: he, she, and the rest of the family could look around and notice, strewn among the stands with their fresh cucumbers and their brightly painted windmills for the front lawn back home, all the other signs along the road.[132]

An advertising executive, looking back on the early years of highway hucksterism, told the story of a young copywriter at a Detroit agency who was sent to New York City for the first time on business. His boss kindly suggested he take the "Water-level Route" *via* Niagara Falls and the Hudson Valley, to enjoy the splendid scenery:

On his return he was asked how the scenic landscape impressed him. "Greatest I ever saw!" was his reply. Asked what impressed him most, he said: "Forty-two

miles of Heinz pickles, fifty-one miles of Burrough's screens, thirty-five miles of Cascarets and eighty-seven miles of Bull Durham tobacco."[133]

In 1925, a young Minneapolis businessman took a long, aimless drive to mull over the problem of trying to sell a new kind of brushless shaving cream, before the stockpiled inventory of Burma-Shave drove his father's firm into bankruptcy. Out of the corner of his eye, Allan Odell glimpsed a series of signs, all extolling the sundry merits of a gas station a little farther up the road. Odell sped back to Minneapolis, invested $200 in a set of wooden signs of his own, and in September of 1926, on U.S. 65 near Lakeville, Minnesota (the main route to Albert Lea!), the first roadside jingle appeared.[134] Further experimentation on U.S. 61 between St. Paul and Red Wing showed that sales boomed when motorists read off the sequence of five jaunty little signs and chortled over the inevitable punch line on the sixth:

> Every Shaver
> Now Can Snore
> Six More Minutes
> Than Before
> By Using
> *Burma-Shave*

By year's end, the signs were dotted across Minnesota, Wisconsin, and Iowa; by 1927, the whole Midwest was watching for the verses by the side of the road. Highway travelers were startled, then delighted, by the serial messages, the phrases of which were planted exactly 100 feet apart. So, at 35 m.p.h., it took some 18 seconds to move from the first sign to the last, completing the commercial. Exacting that much concentrated attention from every literate passerby was regarded in the ad trade as miraculous. As Alexander Wolcott observed, it was harder to pass up a Burma-Shave jingle than it was to eat just one salted peanut.[135] The signs took advantage of the straight, flat, monotonous roads of Allan Odell's native Minnesota. They broke the tedium of the prairie highway with humor and with 500 feet of suspense.

As this parking lot shows, the Wall Drug signs do their job. Photo courtesy of Wall Drug, Wall, South Dakota.

Wall Drug, an altogether unprepossessing establishment on Main Street in the dusty hamlet of Wall, South Dakota, borrowed the suspense of the Burma-Shave signs in the 1930s and prolonged the tension for hundreds of miles. Roadside signs offering a free glass of ice water to all comers blossomed first in Minnesota, Iowa, and Nebraska; every year, they crept farther toward the Atlantic and the Pacific. The signs informed the motorist that however distant his destination might be, Wall Drug was a mere 429 or 387 or 263 miles ahead, and that the wayfarer could view every imaginable marvel of Mid-America therein, while guzzling down gallons of free, pure, icy-cold water. Wall Drug had jackalopes, and a real, 80-foot dinosaur, and a whole lot more.[136] After passing a brace of Wall Drug signs on a hot and treeless road, with nothing to see except the Burma-Shave jingles and fields of corn reaching all the way to the horizons, fore and aft, a stupefying anticipation begins to mount. The miles slip away, faster and faster.

The signs often turn up far from home; in this case, Wall Drug is advertised along a canal in Amsterdam, Holland. T. W. Hogendijk Foto, courtesy of Wall Drug, Wall, South Dakota.

The famous "Spearman" billboard in Times Square, ca. 1935. From a plate in Hugh Agnew, *Outdoor Advertising* (1938).

A local adaptation of the motif, still visible in Stillwater, Minnesota in 1976. Photo by Bruce White.

A Sunkist "iceberg" billboard of the 1930s. From a plate in Hugh Agnew, *Outdoor Advertising* (1938).

We're almost there! In the touristic imagination, Wall Drug becomes Mecca, Nirvana, and Shangri-La. It is a kind of Barnum-in-the-Badlands hoax, a colossal bit of roadside humor.

During the Depression, the homegrown whimsy of midwestern signs was mimicked and intensified. Theorists of the hard sell argued that messages beamed at the motorist called for special, sophisticated techniques of persuasion. Billboards occupied a branch of the science of "Outdoor Advertising," and marketing students were solemnly admonished to learn from the case histories of legendary roadside promotions. The formula for lapel-grabbing salesmanship on the road called for a minimum of text and objects of maximal size, arrayed on billboards of overwhelming scale. The "electrified spectaculars" in Times Square set the benchmark for lesser roadside "bulletins." Biggest and best was the animated Wrigley sign: the little "Spearman" from the gum wrapper, now 30 feet high, swam in slow motion among "gigantic, multi-colored fish . . . [and] waves of sea-green light."

At night, the effect almost stopped traffic, and the use of 29,508 light bulbs was not practical for most signs on U.S. 65, out toward Albert Lea, Minnesota, but the immense size of the trademark and the oddity of the image were readily copied. Sunkist's famous lemonade billboard needed no flashing lights to get its message across: full-color renderings of gigantic icebergs cradling cosmic lemons did the trick. The Sinclair Oil campaign of 1934, 1935, and 1936 carried the drive for bigger, stranger images to extremes, however. The firm had been using a large, green trademark dinosaur of proven memorability on its outdoor ads. The new series aimed to illustrate the power of Sinclair's product by showing how high the energy in a single gallon would lift the S.S. Leviathan, the Empire State Building, or the Statue of Liberty.[137] The picture of the colossal and solemnly classical Liberty, levitating above her base, was a corporate tall tale illustrated. Deliberately bizarre, and hugely grotesque, the sign stood out from the others crowding the streets and roadsides of a modern America on wheels.

The roadside colossus is that kind of monstrous sign. John Margolies, in his photographic study of highway architecture in America, remarks that "the Wall Drug dinosaur has no function but to stand by the interstate as the ultimate billboard, the irresistible last venal gasp."[138] Even in 18th-century America, crowded cities traversed by horse-drawn vehicles often demanded the intrusive, physical bulk of life-sized advertising sculpture in the round to lure trade. By this simple logic, then, the 20th-century colossus—an inflated and diversified cigarstore Indian—would seem responsive to two variable conditions: the rate of speed at which the viewer moves past a given sign, and the spatial characteristics of the environment in which the sign is matrixed.

Historians who have examined American roadside vernacular architecture of the 1920s and 30s have proceeded along these lines. The buildings they illustrate are commercial, responsive initially to the consumerism and the advertising boom of the 1920s and secondarily to the business despair of the 1930s.[139] Some of these oddities rely on architectural conventions, wildly inflated, to call attention to themselves and the product vended. The ubiquitous Wigwam Village Motel-cum-filling station is a good example. Warren Belasco points out that "wandering tourists emulated plains nomads in these tepee huts of the late 30s" outside Bardstown, Kentucky.[140] Margolies and other collectors of highway Americana have found stray survivors of the would-be chain, sometimes turned to other uses, in Allentown, Arizona; Cave City, Kentucky; Rialto, California; and Coulee City, Washington.[141] The tepee, as an Indian relic, is a roadside curiosity and a statement about the frontier status of the highway. As an architectural form, the tepee shape conveys messages of transience, shelter, and temporary stoppage: a scale enlarged beyond the strict functional demands of shelter allows the message to reach the occupants of a car moving at a considerable rate of speed, and at a considerable distance down the road from the motel complex.

A second class of vernacular buildings, like the shell-shaped Shell Oil stations of the 1930s

The Bardstown, Kentucky, wigwams of the 1930s. Photo courtesy of the Library of Congress.

A stray wigwam in Coulee City, Washington, ca. 1939. Dorthea Lange photograph, courtesy of the Library of Congress.

A Shell filling station, Winston-Salem, North Carolina. Photo courtesy of the University of Minnesota Photo Archive.

Patent drawing for an igloo restaurant by J. H. Whitington of Los Angeles in 1928. Photo courtesy of U.S. Patent Office.

An iceberg restaurant in Tulsa, Oklahoma. Photograph ©JOHN MARGOLIES/ESTO.

—one still stands in Winston-Salem, North Carolina—expands a two-dimensional trademark or sign into an arresting three-dimensional sculpture, which is also the locus of the business and its competitive edge over the visual clutter of the street.[142] Were the truly enormous Jolly Green Giant in Blue Earth, Minnesota, hollowed out to accommodate a pea soup emporium, the dynamic might be comparable.[143] Whereas the gas station in a fantastical cockle shell must overcome a blur of curbside distractions, the Jolly Green Giant must compete with the kind of midwestern space novelist O. E. Rolvaag described, but one infinitely complicated by the motorist's modern speed. In *Giants In the Earth*, the plains are a monotonous sea on earth, running "straight toward the west, straight toward the sky line."[144] What is wanted, as in the days when Per Hansa set out from Fillmore County, Minnesota, is a distraction from the stationary horizon line, rendered all the more terrifying when the speedometer of the flivver registers 40 or 50 for several hours. What Per Hansa needed was a tree, a landmark toward which the pioneer in his wagon could pick his way onward. What Rolvaag's motorist-reader of 1927 needed was a landmark of greater magnitude, a stopping point that would validate his belief that he had, in fact, moved from back there to a fixed, identifiable place, interposed between his starting point—or past—and a destination that fled ever before him into the future. The landmark is a frontier; and that frontier creates the fleeting and comforting illusion of a stable present, the illusion of a now.

The roadside colossi of the Midwest are, it would seem, close relatives of that Shell station on the half-shell and kissin' cousins of a third category of vernacular buildings shaped into giant people, animals, architectural forms, and other objects that are not, or were not, recognized trademarks. Unlike the Wigwam Villages, the igloos, icebergs, and ice palaces of the late 1920s still standing in Los Angeles and Tulsa do not directly invoke a correlation between aboriginal shelter and rooms for overnight guests. Any statement about shelter is made by reversal, by tacit contrast with the openness and heat of the road: stop, come inside, and cool off! Unlike the Shell station, iceberg shapes do not identify a specific product: as Eskimo pies dance unbidden before his mind's eye, the sweaty motorist hopes for ice cream of any variety, for cold drinks aplenty, for air conditioning.

What commentators fail to detect in their analyses of the icebergs, however, is that they are landmarks that willfully distort or dissolve the errant roadside locale their arresting forms seem to grip fast and identify.[145] In effect, these structures *mis*identify California and Oklahoma as the frozen northland, a place given special character and identity by "The Ice Palace" of F. Scott Fitzgerald's 1920 short story. At the end of World War I, the hero brings his Southern fiancée home during the dead of winter and boasts of his city's cold weather attractions:

> "It's carnival time, you know. First in ten years. And there's an ice palace they're building now that's the first they've had since eighty-five. Built out of blocks of the clearest ice they could find—on a tremendous scale. . . . It's a hundred and seventy feet tall . . . covers six thousand square yards."[146]

The great size of the building is as important to Sally Carrol's fictional suitor as it was, in reality, to the St. Paul boosters who founded the Winter Carnival in 1886, and a St. Paul Winter Carnival compounded of a little recent fact and a little historical fancy is the setting for Fitzgerald's story. The Carnival was the local rejoinder to the jibe of an Eastern journalist who had compared Minnesota's capital unfavorably with Siberia:

> The ice palace was a symbol of civic pride. It made a virtue out of St. Paul's long, cold winter—the very factor that allowed the city to produce such a thing as an ice palace in the first place. And the early palaces were meant to attract huge crowds, as many as 30,000 people.[147]

Postcard view of the Saint Paul Winter Carnival Ice Palace, 1941 edition. From a Mando Post Card Service postcard.

A day scene, showing rusticated detail. From a Mando Post Card Service postcard.

Fireworks over the Ice Palace are depicted in the background of this 1916 scene, the cover of a piece of sheet music. From a design by the Engraving Company for Landman and Wessel, Music Publishers, St. Paul.

But regardless of the size of the crowds to be accommodated, the aesthetic of the tall tale mandated immense ice palaces to illustrate the gargantuan proportions of St. Paul's boastful mastery of the elements. The weather stories Minnesotans tell today still run to extremes of cold and wind, extremes symbolized by the towering palaces of ice. Tourist bureaus and economic development offices may cringe at the uninviting image conveyed abroad by this local variant on the fish story, but a collective sense of living in a place of big challenges routinely met by the grandiose force of native character is basic to the regional identity. The frontier hardships of yore are still spectacularly real in a midwestern culture that remains fettered to the elements by the bonds of agribusiness and tourism.

What a tourist might make of the St. Paul Winter Carnival is one theme of Fitzgerald's story. Natives tell Sally Carrol that if she's never seen a lot of snow, "it'll be like a fairyland to you," crowned by a fairy-tale castle of "opalescent, translucent ice."[148] The buildings Fitzgerald describes are the spectacular castles of 1886, 1887, and 1888, with their romantic turrets and lofty battlements; half-hearted attempts to revive the ice palace tradition in 1916 and 1917 produced stubby forts that merely defined the area in which carnival events would take place. They did not have the glistening interior labyrinths where Sally Carrol is trapped in a memory recreated by St. Paul only in 1937, when the largest ice palace to date arose to compete with the enormous statue of Paul Bunyan and with the Paul Bunyan Winter Carnival in Bemidji.

Long before 1937, to be sure, Sally Carrol had gone back to Georgia, her alienation from the ways of the North symbolized by her harrowing entombment in the cold and lovely towers of the fairy-castle in St. Paul. Fitzgerald understands "The Ice Palace" as a fragile fantasy, like love itself, and a place marker, standing for the manners and mores endemic to a particular locale. As roadside place markers, however, the misplaced igloos of Los Angeles and Tulsa correspond more closely to Eckleburg's eyes in the valley of ashes, suspending reality at the frontier of unbounded fantasy. Like Alice's rabbit hole, the igloo is the point of magical passage along a dreamlike road that wends its way out of real time and space, into the realm of the imagination.

Among the buildings-turned-sculptures of this ilk that have severed all ties to architectural conventions are the California mega-oranges and lemons of the 1920s; the Harlingen, Texas, pig, and the Lane, Oregon, dog of 1939 (both anticipated by comparable California beasts of the 1920s); the Sphinx Realty office of 1926 in Los Angeles; and Mammy's Cupboard, also known as "The Mammy Station," outside Natchez, Mississippi.[149] The last-named, in her present form, is not precisely dated: her skirt opened for business in 1939 but her earrings and tray are later embellishments. Nonetheless, patent applications for skirted buildings—as well as for buildings shaped like airplanes, dirigibles, fish, lunch pails, ears of corn, and coffeepots—appear almost a decade earlier.[150] Mammy and her cohorts are close contemporaries of Doctor T. J. Eckleburg and Paul Bunyan.

The lemon-shaped lemonade stands endemic to California are, in some ways, the three-dimensional equivalents of the printed ads for Adams California Tutti-Frutti Gum or the giant, illuminated billboards for Sunkist lemonade. The outlandish scale of the lemon peddles the product and by shrinking the rest of reality into insignificance makes fruit the singular focus of consumer lust. But it is one thing to encounter an image of a pack of fruit gum rendered as large as an adjacent person within the fictional conventions of pictorial art, and quite another to belly up to an orange or a lemon the size of a small bungalow. In this instance, the customer is not expected to wallow in, through giant seeds and pulp strings, as she must enter the ice cream igloo through a papier-mâché snow tunnel: indeed, she is debarred from doing so. At the same time, however, awareness that this piece of hollow fruit is comparable to normative modes of shelter can scarcely be avoided, and with awareness comes a sense of fantasy, a release from all operative norms.

The Lane, Oregon, dog, ca. 1939. Dorthea Lange photograph, courtesy of the Library of Congress.

Mammy's Cupboard, Natchez, Mississippi. Photograph ©JOHN MARGOLIES/ESTO.

A lemonade stand in California, ca. 1926. Photo courtesy of the National Archives.

Mother Goose Pantry Restaurant, Pasadena, California, 1929. Photo courtesy of the National Archives.

The Harlingen, Texas, pig, ca. 1939. Russell Lee photograph, courtesy of the Library of Congress.

One of the Barkies' Sandwich Shops, Los Angeles, 1930. Photo courtesy of the National Archives.

The lemon is the botanical equivalent of the Old Woman's capacious nursery-rhyme shoe, and naturally enough a Mother Goose Pantry Restaurant planted "the largest insole in the world" on Colorado Boulevard in Pasadena in 1929. As an advertising specialist noted with undisguised admiration in 1931, the road "is lined with wayside places of various types and designs for miles. Every one of these is forgotten, however, save the famous Mother Goose Pantry [in a shoe]. . . . No human being with a fraction of imagination could forget the Mother Goose Pantry."[151] Nathaniel West, for one, could not forget that shoe. In *The Day of the Locust*, he reimagined the Mother Goose Pantry as "the 'Cinderella Bar,' a little stucco building in the shape of a lady's slipper, on Western Avenue. Its floor show consisted of female impersonators."[152]

The architecture of fantasy always sells illusions, along with drinks and ice cream and hot dogs. The lemons in the shadow of California's citrus groves dispensed lemonade. The Texas pig dispensed pork bar-b-que—what *Fortune* called "the roadside name for . . . roast meat," an exotic word, shortened to connote speed on the open road. When *Fortune* tried to determine just where the $7 per diem spent by each vacationing motorist went, it proved impossible to draw a firm line between the $1.47 spent for restaurant meals, the 42 cents for "candy, ice cream, hot dogs, and similar roe," and the 56 cents for places of amusement: roadside drive-ins shaped like ice cream buckets or fish or pigs seemed to fit all those categories at once. Wayside stops promised food, and some ineffable something more besides.[153]

Mammy Gas, for example, hinted broadly at southern hospitality, at cavalier memories of childhood comforts. Like Robert Venturi's paradigmatic Long Island duckling store in Riverhead, New York, the building-turned-colossus is a sign.[154] But the product symbolism, complicated even when it seems most obvious, is occasionally opaque. The Oregon dog bore no attendant billboards suggesting hot dogs for sale, and seems to have specialized in sandwiches and coffee. The whimsical connec-

A postcard shot of the Long Island duck. From a Tomlin Art Company (Islip, New York) postcard, with an original color photograph by Milt Price.

tion between Fido and fast food sometimes essayed in hot dog stands of the 1930s skirted consumer nausea by linking canine sculpture with the coy names of the restaurants (for example, "Barkies' Sandwiches" or "Tail o' the Pup"), not with their bills of fare.

Sphinx Realty lacked even that minimal concession to sober salesmanship. The company, apparently, sold neither cemetery plots nor spaces in Forest Lawn, and no more than its share of arid building lots in sunbaked subdivisions. Rather than a building warped into a colossal figure, this is a preexisting colossal statue, first shrunken in size and then scooped out to form a building. The content of the signage or symbolism, on both practical and aesthetic levels, is hopelessly cloudy. The passerby might easily postulate that Sphinx Realty is an ancient and therefore an honorable firm, or, conversely, that it is a trendy Egyptomaniac's answer to King Tut's recently discovered tomb, filtered through the Hollywood neo-Arabianism of Valentino and Theda Bara.[155] Whatever the intention, the Los Angeles Sphinx is as freakish and enigmatic a presence as its famous prototype.

The Day of the Locust is fundamentally concerned with the enigma of a Los Angeles of roadside sphinxes, a city that feeds on the mammoth hoax of Hollywood. The last frontier, the place where all roads west must end, California marks the farthest, sun-blurred boundary between illusion and reality. It is the place where dreams come to die. And so West's novel ends with an apocalyptic vision of "The Burning of Los Angeles," the theme of a picture dreamed of but never painted by his hero, Tod Hackett, a would-be artist, now a studio set designer. Ironically, the vision was Hollywood's before it was Tod's. In 1933, *King Kong* thrilled movie-goers by simulating the destruction of a mighty city at the gigantic hands of a creature from the land of the dinosaurs, beyond the western sea.[156]

On a backlot in California, Kong ravaged New York City, and the sight of a 50-foot monster clinging to the finial of the Empire State Building was the kind of miraculous illusion the bored fans of *The Day of the Locust*

Sphinx Realty, Los Angeles, 1926. Note pyramid- and camel-shaped billboards at left. United Press International Photo; all rights reserved.

A publicity still advertising *King Kong*, who towers over the Empire State Building. From a poster published by RKO Pictures.

demanded. When reality cannot match what Hollywood promises, the dreamers despair and a riot erupts at a film premiere. The riot is too real: dream becomes nightmare as Tod sees his canvas in his mind's eye, and drawn upon it "a great bonfire of architectural styles, ranging from Egyptian to Cape Cod colonial." The bonfire incinerates the flimsy, make-believe suburbs of Los Angeles, but the picture also harks back to the pivotal image of the novel, Tod Hackett's nightmarish trek across the studio backlot. Under a blazing sun, he stumbles through a western saloon that becomes a jungle and a Paris street and a Greek temple:

> The only bit of shade he could find was under an ocean liner made of painted canvas with real life boats hanging from the davits. He stood in its narrow shadow for a while, then went toward a great forty-foot papier-mâché sphinx that loomed up in the distance. . . . He pushed his way through a tangle of briars, old flats and iron junk, skirting the skeleton of a Zeppelin, a bamboo stockade, an adobe fort, the wooden horse of Troy, a flight of baroque palace stairs that started in a bed of weeds and ended against the branches of an oak, part of the Fourteenth Street elevated station, a Dutch windmill, the bones of a dinosaur, the upper half of the Merrimac, a corner of a Mayan temple, until he finally reached the road.[157]

As a refuse truck adds another load to the gigantic pile of sets and props, Tod Hackett and the phony Sphinx brood blindly over the desolate scene:

> This was the final dumping ground. . . . A Sargasso of the imagination! And the dump grew continually, for there wasn't a dream afloat somewhere which wouldn't sooner or later turn up on it, having first been made photographic by plaster, canvas, lath and paint. Many boats sink and never reach the Sargasso, but no dream entirely disappears.[158]

The final resting place of Fitzgerald's orgiastic dream, that "dumping ground" is an obvious reprise of the "valley of ashes" in *The Great Gatsby*. The last frontier is just as illusory and elusive as the first. Across a continent, a vision unseen by sightless eyes answers a riddle unspoken by a silent Sphinx. Twin colossi mark the place where the dream begins, beyond the litter of the city, on "the fresh green breast of a new world" rolling west, and the place where it plays itself out, in a heap of trash at the end of America. Eckleburg's titanic eyes and the "great forty-foot papier-mâché" California Sphinx preside over the debris of a trashy, commercial culture, to which they are eminently suitable monuments.

SCALE, PATRIOTISM, AND FUN
Crossing the Last Frontier of Fantasy

According to the rhetoric of a debate that erupted in Germany in 1933 under the leadership of Hermann Broch and was brought to a raging boil in America by Clement Greenberg in 1939, the California Sphinx is a prime example of "kitsch."[159] In its most restrained definition, the verb "kitschen" means to produce trash, or fake art, by manipulating real art, especially the art of past ages, in the manufacture of articles for mass consumption.[160] In the practice of the late 1930s, however, kitsch came to mean the antithesis of elite, high culture, particularly artifacts deviating from the canons of avant-garde art and architecture. Whereas Broch had conceded that "there is a drop of kitsch in all art," the term signified bad taste, blatant excess, and a tinge of pornography, all relative judgments, to be sure, calibrated against the prevailing tenets of a highly serious, chastened modernism. Essentially, then, the most damnable quality of kitsch was its popular origin and its hard-to-define but unquestionable appeal to mass culture.

"Kitsch is art that follows established rules at a time when all rules in art are put into question by each artist," wrote Harold Rosenberg, dean of the formalists:

Kitsch is the daily art of our time, as the vase or the hymn was for earlier generations. For the sensibility it has that arbitrariness and importance which works take on when they are no longer noticeable elements of the environment. In America kitsch is nature. The Rocky Mountains have resembled fake art for a century. There is no counterconcept to kitsch. Its antagonist is not an idea but reality. To do away with kitsch it is necessary to change the landscape, as it was necessary to change the landscape of Sardinia to get rid of the malarial mosquito.[161]

The vernacular California Sphinx is an affront to art because it recreates a masterwork; it copies, it "follows the established rules" at a time when the avant-garde pursued a course of idiosyncratic individualism. The rule of modernism is to assault the rule of rule. But for all its obeisance to historical rule, the Sphinx is as startlingly idiosyncratic as any Jackson Pollock (or John Marin, or Gerald Murphy), precisely because it does *not* exist in a "daily" environment. In the world of North Fairfax Boulevard in 1926 (or in 1984), it does not behave like a vase or a hymn, providing visual background music for daily activities. Its arbitrariness and self-importance impinge on and alter the workaday environment. A modest street address becomes the site of endless questioning and an endless variety of illogical, imaginative, fantastic answers to the riddle of this Sphinx.

Although appalled and angered by the very mention of kitsch, Rosenberg has several cogent insights to offer on its American manifestations. The antagonist of kitsch is, as he correctly implies, the reality of Los Angeles, not the ideology of modern art, and the environment—nature in America—is the focus of this persistent drive to step beyond the frontier of reality into the fantasyland of the imagination. In Rosenberg's lexicon the gigantic Rockies are, *per se*, kitsch—obvious, blatant, excessive, semipornographic. That set of adjectives can be conflated into one, gigantic "too muchness." Nature made an aesthetic error of scale in America, troublesome to art critics, mythmakers, landscape painters, tricksters, novelists, and tourists ever since.

Between 1927 and 1939, Gutzon Borglum set out to rectify that mistake in the Black Hills, by turning Mt. Rushmore, South Dakota, into the largest statue in the world, a set of portrait busts of four presidents unfailingly cited in handbooks of kitsch alongside the Statue of Liberty, a French gift to the United States, unveiled in 1886, but thereafter blamed

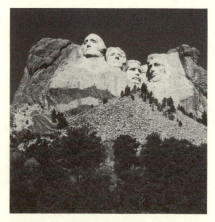

Borglum's Mount Rushmore, in the Black Hills of South Dakota, begun in 1927. Photo courtesy of South Dakota Tourism.

The Statue of Liberty, 152 feet tall, was dedicated in 1886. Richard Frear photograph, courtesy of the National Park Service, U. S. Department of the Interior.

exclusively on American bad taste.[162] Kitsch or not, Mt. Rushmore is a stunningly successful attempt to turn reality on its ear. A mountain becomes a statue. By carving Mt. Rushmore, man takes over the shaping role of nature and tailors the physical environment to his own measure. The activity humbles nature and renders it responsive to human control.

In literal terms, Borglum reenacted the metaphorical task of W. B. Laughead, Ned Buntline, and Davy Crockett: he made frontier giants of stone, fully as large as the continent. Borglum had been born in the spacious frontier country near the border of Idaho and Nevada, and from the beginning of his noisy career, aimed at a grandiose scale derived, he said, "from American sources, memorializing American achievement." Thus he despised the genteel reticence of official U.S. classicism. The little temple on the Potomac dedicated to Lincoln in 1922 had nothing to do with the robust essence of the man. As for the marble obelisk of the Washington Monument, "if there weren't a policeman to tell you that [it] was placed there to record the work and life of a man who built this great nation after eight years of one of the most trying wars that a little people ever had," could a stranger from "Timbuctoo" deduce the meaning of that pallid shaft? The American story, Borglum argued, was bigger and earthier than art had hitherto cared to admit: "There was never a better one lived. We have had all the emotions any people on the earth ever had," and at a pitch of intensity Borglum would translate into stupefying size.[163]

In 1913, the United Daughters of the Confederacy invited Borglum to submit designs for a bas-relief of Robert E. Lee to be carved into the living rock on the face of Stone Mountain, in Georgia. The overall dimensions contemplated for the bust were based on those of Thorvaldsen's *Lion of Lucerne*. In other words, as Borglum later recalled their invitation, the ladies' timid plan—more European than American—was to "subordinate it wholly to the space upon which it was to be placed, . . . a great granite facade eight hundred feet in height and about three thousand feet in

length."[164] Instead, Gutzon Borglum conceived
of a design covering the whole mountainside
with a procession of Confederate chieftains, led
by a full-length figure of the general so immense that "a workman engaged in chiselling
the hat will appear from below no larger than
a fly." An advocate presenting the project to a
businessmen's meeting stunned his audience
when he announced that a work of such magnitude would cost the city of Atlanta 50 million
dollars:

> There was a chorus of exclamations and
> questions, but the speaker went on, "It
> will cost the city as much as that to build
> new roads and erect hotels, to care for the
> tourists who will come to see Stone
> Mountain."[165]

The artist was not insensitive to the publicity value of his epochal stunt, nor did he
sneeze at tourism. Having grasped that the
sheer hubris of his determination to carve
Stone Mountain was raising eyebrows well
beyond Atlanta, however, Borglum was hard
pressed to give his essentially southern
memorial a broader and a bigger meaning. In
interviews, he began speaking of his mountain
as "a symbol, in really American dimensions, of
a vital chapter in our history—a symbol of
the union of all the forces which make for the
greatness of our nation."[166] Granting that the
Civil War had been a watershed in national
history, cooler heads wondered whether the
lost Confederate cause merited the immortality
of the Rock of Ages:

> No one will quarrel with Mr. Borglum's
> audacity in seizing the opportunity to
> sign his name, in letters fifty feet high, to
> the largest monument in the world, bar
> none. Nothing has ever been attempted
> on this scale before, either in ancient
> Egypt or Assyria. The Colossus of
> Rhodes wasn't anywhere near eight
> hundred feet high, that is certain. . . .
> [Borglum] admits that already there is a
> fifty-thousand-dollar oiled road to the
> base of his potential monument. One

wonders did the Pharaohs erect road houses furnishing excellent chicken dinners at the feet of their pyramids to attract camel-touring parties?[167]

At first, Borglum's enthusiasm silenced the doubters. His plans were adopted and the site was solemnly dedicated in May of 1916. Although work was suspended during the war, blasting resumed in the fall of 1922. On January 19, 1924, Lee's head was unveiled: the occasion was marked by a formal luncheon served on a table mounted on the general's shoulder. Borglum had finished the trifle his patrons had wanted in the first place, but that very measure of accomplishment revealed the lifetime of work ahead. Promoters cooled toward Stone Mountain, there was little for tourists to see, funds ran short, and the sculptor squabbled with all concerned. In 1925, Borglum was summarily dismissed and then arrested for destroying the models others might have used to complete his mountainside monument.[168] While some southern newspapers hoped that the artist's temperamental outbursts would be overlooked, other teetered between apathy and outright antipathy because, as the Norfolk *Virginia-Pilot* put it, "there still clings to the enterprise, despite its sincerely patriotic conception, an odor of Babbittic Atlanta advertising and the handicap of a fortuitous but highly unfortunate association with the Ku Klux Klan, which claims Stone Mountain as its holy birthplace and Atlanta as its holy city." As a landmark calculated to make "Atlanta a Mecca for tourists of all nations," Stone Mountain was foredoomed. Although Borglum called his Confederate Valhalla "an idea as deep, as basic as the rocks upon which our wonderful Continent rests," the theme was meaningless to many Americans, and odious to others. The idea of a sculpted mountain was indeed compelling and "basic," but the Confederate Monument carved on Stone Mountain was a barrier between the South and the nation at large.[169]

Amid the accusations and recriminations came a letter from South Dakota, inviting Borglum to tour the Black Hills "to see if a mountain monument to America's greatness could be carved there." The sculptor arrived in September of 1925 with his 12-year-old son, Lincoln, in tow: they never left the granite heights of Cathedral Cliff again. It is clear that Borglum was deeply affected by the overwhelming size of his new site. "The vastness that lay here," he confessed to his journal, "demanded complete remodelling of the grouping I had been dreaming. I must see, think, feel and draw in Thor's dimension."[170] It is also clear that the size of the mountain turned his thoughts toward grander themes, of national resonance and popular accessibility. So, too, did his appraisal of the changing scale of modern life:

> Everything in modern civilization has so expanded that the very scale, the breadth of one's thought, is no longer limited by town, city, county, or state. . . . I believe it was natural and consistent with the great modern awakening that I should have turned to the huge cliffs of our land, the lofty granite ledges, and in them carve monuments and there leave records of the founding of our great nation and the development of our civilization.[171]

Borglum's own contemporaneity was never in doubt. He took the first chunk out of Mount Rushmore in 1927. As work speeded up with the introduction of jackhammers and new methods of dynamite sculpting, however, a columnist for *The Nation* admitted to a certain apprehension about what fully mechanized mankind might do to the landscape:

> To come face to face with Washington or Lincoln along some remote mountain range would be at least bearable. But [I] cannot face the prospect of having to pitch . . . camp under the nose of Henry Ford.[172]

Insofar as Borglum's monument reflected a restless, tourist culture, roaming the continent by automobile in search of sensations to match the force of its dreams, Henry Ford might well

These are frontier presidents, and colossi marking the last American frontier. The faces were carved to the scale of men 465 feet tall. Richard Frear photograph, courtesy of the National Park Service, U. S. Department of the Interior.

have joined his company of heroes as a presiding deity. Atop the rugged peaks where the West begins, Borglum dominated the wilderness with his blasting caps and his modern optimism; he asserted his absolute mastery over the frontier, subjugating it in the act of carving the mountain. Borglum became another Paul Bunyan of the 1920s and 30s, and lived out the frontier tradition of the tall tale.

The iconography of Mt. Rushmore reinforces the meaning of this act of conquest. Mountain is man and the men depicted are the pathfinders, the explorers, the tamers of the frontier. Washington surveyed the Western Reserve. Jefferson dispatched Lewis and Clark to the Louisiana Territory. Lincoln, the railsplitter, was the rawboned son of the western border. "T. R.," the roughrider, the expansionist, founded the cult of the strenuous life on the high plains of the Dakota Territory. They are frontier presidents, who claimed and reclaimed that frontier dream of perpetual movement, escape, and self-transformation in the name of the American nation. They symbolize the American rite of passage, and defiantly

anchored by Borglum in 1927 at the demo-
graphic edge of civilization, Mt. Rushmore is
itself a perpetual frontier, an emblematic gateway leading to our historical dreams and so to
the "dark fields of the republic," rolling ever
westward, backward in time and forward in
space.[173]

Borglum's landmark gave physical definition to the dream of westering. A pair of very
different monuments of the same vintage,
erected in downtown Minneapolis and downtown St. Paul, also located the frontier with the
vehemence of colossal size. The head of George
Washington on Mount Rushmore was unveiled
in 1930. In 1929, a 447-foot free copy of the
Washington Monument, enlarged to contain a
32-story office building, opened on Marquette
Avenue in Minneapolis. The design was an
unusual marriage of historical imagery with
modern utility, the latter given symbolic expression in the streamlined, Art Deco details of
the decor. For that reason alone, the sculpture
cum skyscraper functioned as a significant if
somewhat grotesque national landmark.[174]
Hailed for a generation as the tallest man-made
structure between Chicago and the Pacific, the
Foshay Tower commemorated the first frontier
and articulated the modern edge of urbanism,
beyond which a western wilderness still lay in
wait for the sturdy adventurer driving to Yellowstone along the route of the pioneers.

St. Paul's colossus was a 36-foot tall *God of
Peace* that rose a full three stories above the
foyer of the City Hall and Court House building on Kellogg Boulevard, and spun about, the
better to amaze the tourists, on the latest word
in motorized bases. The statue was conceived
as a veterans' memorial and commissioned in
1932 from Carl Milles, a Swedish artist whose
"moderne" design ostensibly depicts the smoke
from native peace pipes congealing into the
milky likeness of a mythological chieftain, the
patron of peaceful pursuits. The specific icono-
graphic connections between local veterans and
the 60-ton lump of white onyx in City Hall
remained obscure. Connections between Minnesota's territorial past and "The World's
Largest Indian" were not.[175] Like the largest
pumpkin awarded the blue ribbon at the Min-

Foshay Tower, 1926-1929, a
447-foot, 32-story skyscraper on
Marquette Avenue in downtown
Minneapolis. A free copy of the
Washington Monument, the building
had no sooner opened—20,000
spectators attended the gala and John
Philip Sousa supplied the music—
than Wilbur Foshay went bankrupt.
In 1932, he was sent to Leavenworth
for mail fraud. Photo by Bruce
White.

Carl Milles's *God of Peace* in Saint
Paul City Hall weighs 60 tons and
rotates 66 degrees left and right of
center every 2½ hours. Photo by
Bruce White.

This 184-pound pumpkin took the prize at the Minnesota State Fair in 1982. Photo by Bruce White.

The larger of these pumpkins weighed 189 pounds and the picture appeared in a booklet prepared by the State of Minnesota for distribution at the St. Louis World's Fair of 1904. From *Minnesota, Brief Sketches of Its History, Resources and Opportunities* (1904).

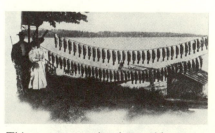

This same promotional pamphlet presented this as a typical day's catch at Geneva Beach, near Alexandria. From *Minnesota, Brief Sketches of Its History, Resources and Opportunities* (1904).

nesota State Fair, "The World's Largest Indian" betokened an expansive local pride and a swelling optimism well suited to the cheerful rhetoric of the New Deal. The fiercely modern style of "Onyx John" measured the distance between the old frontier of Indian times and a machine-driven tomorrow, the frontier of the streamlined, aerodynamic future toward which the rocketing profile of the Foshay Tower beckoned, too.

Mt. Rushmore, South Dakota, shares the midwestern environment of "The World's Largest Indian," Bemidji's Paul Bunyan, and other tall tales writ taller still. The Statue of Liberty inhabits the eastern terrain of Eckleburg's eyes above Queens. Marvin Trachtenberg has noted that the siting of the Statue of Liberty in New York Harbor is ambiguous. From the deck of an arriving ship, Liberty is a beacon of welcome and enlightenment. In the words of "The New Colossus," the Emma Lazarus poem inscribed on her base, Liberty "lifts her lamp beside the Golden Door." From the shoreline, however, Liberty seems to turn her back on the immigrant and the Old World; indeed, she seems to stride west, casting her beams of enlightenment over the dark frontier unrolling before her, toward Minnesota and the Dakotas.[176] But, to "wretched refuse" and native son alike, Liberty marks a door, a place of potential transfiguration. In common with Eckleburg's eyes, the colossus defines a frontier between factual reality and the imaginatively conceived, dream America beyond the border stele. On the other side of the "Golden Door," the pioneer, the dreamer, the quester, the seeker, and the wandering pilgrim step out of time and circumstance into the dazzling radiance of their own last, best hopes.

Gatsby and Nick Carraway cross Eckleburg's frontier repeatedly in Fitzgerald's novel, the former as blind to its significance as the sightless signboard and the latter gradually opening his eyes to the delights and terrors of revelation. In moments of anxiety, Gatsby shuns the valley of ashes; instead, he asks Nick to go with him to Coney Island or Atlantic City, spawning grounds of the American popular colossus. On the road to Atlantic City, one

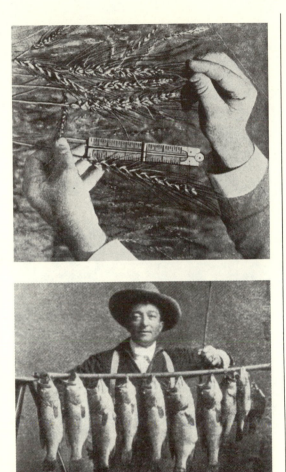

The size of hybrid wheat grown in the state was also stressed. From *Minnesota, Brief Sketches of Its History, Resources and Opportunities* (1904).

The Minnesota State Board of Immigration labeled this picture "An Hour's Catch at Amber Lake, Martin County." From *Minnesota's Fiftieth Anniversary*, undated, 4th edition.

"Fairchild," a colossal gopher, is the official mascot of the Minnesota State Fair. His size is appropriate to the emphasis on large scale in the farm machinery and agricultural products exhibited. Photo by Bruce White.

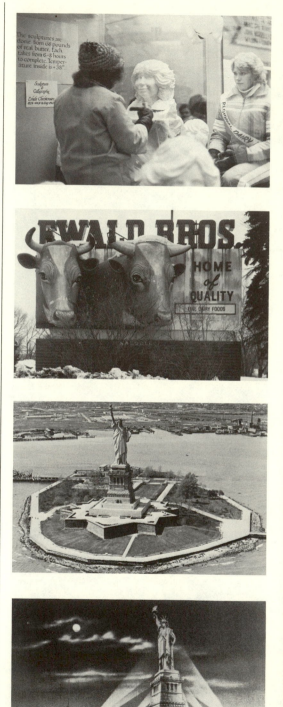

Butter sculptures exhibited and made at the Minnesota State Fair every year are no larger than life; they do, however, use massive quantities of foodstuffs, and subject both sitter and sculptor to dramatic extremes of temperature in midsummer. This picture was taken in the Dairy Building in 1978, but the ritual has changed little since. Photo by Bruce White.

This sign, once in Golden Valley, Minnesota, has been moved to the entrance of the State Fairgrounds. The scale of the cows makes it an appropriate symbol for Minnesota agriculture and for the exuberant spirit of the fair. Photo by Bruce White.

The Statue of Liberty in New York Harbor. Richard Frear photograph, courtesy of the National Park Service, U. S. Department of the Interior.

A dramatic postcard rendering of Miss Liberty, ca. 1940. From an Irving Underhill/Curteich postcard.

"Lucy," the Margate Elephant, near Atlantic City, New Jersey. From a Jack Freeman, Inc. (Longport, New Jersey) postcard.

James V. Lafferty, between 1881 and 1885, built Lucy, the Margate Elephant. In a bizarre presentiment of the Los Angeles Sphinx, Lucy was built to house a real estate office, although she has also served as a flophouse, a tourist information booth, a children's library, and, for the past several years, as a landmark on the National Register of Historic Places.[177] The records are silent on the fate of the real estate firm; the 65-foot Lucy herself, however, was a huge success. Within the decade Lafferty had built another at Cape May, New Jersey, and a third on Coney Island.[178]

The Coney Island elephant was larger, "as big as a church," and was intended to be a resort hotel. "Its legs were 60 feet in circumference. In one front leg was a cigar store, in the other a diorama; patrons walked up circular steps in one hind leg and down the other."[179] Rooms could be had in thigh, shoulder, hip or trunk. After dark, searchlights flashed erratically from the eyes, illuminating anyone within range who had decided to settle for a parsimonious night on the beach.

Lucy's eyes were a simple commercial come-on. But her circus body signaled fun afoot, a

Bird's eye view of Coney Island, ca. 1890, showing the Elephant Hotel. Anonymous photograph, courtesy of the Museum of the City of New York, New York.

This "Lucy" stands alongside the Cletus P. Dunn Service Station on Highway 61 in Saint Paul, Minnesota. The late Mr. Dunn erected a group of animal and fairytale statues on the lot between the station and his house in the 1950s to keep kids out of the road; one of his own children had been killed in a traffic accident on the spot. Photo by Bruce White.

Colossi are often identified with resort hotels even today. These Indians—one posed in a manner suggestive of the Statue of Liberty— are part of the "atmospheric" roadside decor of the Thunderbird Motel in Bloomington, Minnesota. Photo by Bruce White.

tourist's adventure amongst Barnum's curiosities. That the form of the elephant-hotel symbolized release from the fetters of convention and routine is demonstrated by John Kasson's observation that "the phrase 'seeing the elephant,' often accompanied by a broad wink, became a euphemism for illicit pleasures."[180] At the deepest and crudest level, the bedrooms and stairways inside invoked the psychic transformation of a Jonah in the belly of the beast, Pinocchio in the innards of a whale. Commercial postcards sold in tourist meccas of the day often depict colossal objects and figures containing pleasure pavilions miniaturized within them: a typical postcard, dated to 1908 and bearing the legend "Greetings from Atlantic City," shows the famous Heinz amusement pier matrixed within a giant pickle, a specific business reference neatly merged with the more generic and fantastic resonance of the image.[181]

With the advent of the automobile, roadside colossi became the pictorial staples of the postcard industry. Symbols of the pleasure trip and the adventure of the open road, the linen-finish postcards of the 1920s and 30s used jangling colors and settings airbrushed clean of everyday clutter to dramatize the already fantastic appearance of Mammy Gas, Toto's Zeppelin Diner and Cocktail Lounge outside Northampton, Massachusetts, a Wigwam Cafe in Browning, Montana, or the Teapot, a postcard, souvenir, and hot dog stand in Chester, West Virginia.[182] And if travel on the interstate is no longer the fabulous odyssey implied by such pictorial fish stories, the Rexall souvenirs, the gas station mementos, and the slick Kodachrome postcards of today still fasten on a Jolly Green Giant, a giant loon, or a Paul Bunyan who wears a size 73 shirt to define the process of "having a wonderful time."

Having a wonderful time on the Boardwalk meant rubbernecking at the third version of Lucy, the elephant-hotel, and any number of other Coney Island colossi and near colossi. The Inexhaustible Cow was a particular favorite in the 1890s. It was a machine constructed "to satisfy the insatiable thirst of visitors" and then disguised as a heroically proportioned bossy. Promoters argued that its milk was

Atlantic City's Heinz Pier inside a pickle—a fantasy postcard of 1908. From a Souvenir Post Card Co. (New York) postcard.

This postcard hits the high spots of Blue Earth and dramatizes the Giant by the nighttime illumination. From a Chamber of Commerce postcard, original photographs by Gary T. Sands.

Colossi and other outsized objects figure prominently among the attractions of Minnesota summarized on this postcard. From an NMN, Inc. (Crosslake, Minnesota) postcard.

Colossi also figure in the design of Minnesota souvenirs. Here, a typical tourist's haul. Photo by Liz Harrison.

"superior to the natural product in the regularity and predictability of its flow, its hygienic quality and its controllable temperature."[183] Artifice was superior to nature—safer, more dependable, richer, less apt to disappoint.

The huge figures that marked the entrances to "Dreamland" and the other rides and attractions at turn-of-the-century Coney Island made the same promise. The dreamland just past the colossus at the ticket window was a better place, full of fun, adventure, and happiness, all conducted in a controlled environment of make-believe, wherein the tourist was guaranteed the pleasures life often denied, and a dream life could be lived out in a perfect, predictable safety real life could seldom provide.[184]

The fantasy colossus has been the visual

Coney Island's "Dreamland." Photo courtesy of the Brooklyn Collection, Brooklyn Public Library, Brooklyn, New York.

trademark of the fair, the carnival, and the amusement park since 1881. "Dreamland" was reincarnated on the Pike at the St. Louis World's Fair under the title of "Creation." A colossal and scantily draped angel – or was she a winged Eve? – enticed the fairgoer to board "a boat that bears him gently away through a labyrinth of underground passages with clever scenery . . . from remote parts of the world. When he disembarks with a sense of having made a voyage," a serious narration from the Book of Genesis was, somehow, anticlimactic. The "Hereafter" attraction, entered under the gaze of an enormous winged sphinx, offered a similar tour of the horrors and thrills of hell, and the "Temple of Mirth," prefaced by a gigantic winking clown and four grinning maidens, sent customers on a voyage through a mirrored maze and shot them back to real life on a circular slide.[185] The Joy Zone at the Panama-Pacific Exposition was a kind of parody of the heroic gigantism of the "serious" buildings, and the inflated industrial propaganda of "serious" exhibits. Underwood displayed a typewriter 15 feet high and 21 feet

Almost identical to Coney Island's "Dreamland," the portals of "Creation" at the St. Louis World's Fair were guarded by a winged female colossus, daringly undraped. From an original photograph by the Official Photograph Company, St. Louis, Missouri.

The doorway to "Hereafter" in St. Louis, with a huge Sphinx. From an original photograph by the Official Photograph Company, St. Louis, Missouri.

Above the "Temple of Mirth" on the Pike, a huge clown with movable eyes drew a crowd in 1904. From an original photograph by the Official Photograph Company, St. Louis, Missouri.

Souvenir postcards from both coasts highlighted the huge World's Fair cash register in 1939. From a souvenir packet manufactured by Stanley A. Piltz Co. and distributed by Pacific Stationers (San Francisco, California).

wide that weighed 14 tons; New York State showed an 11-thousand-pound cheese. The amusement concessionaires responded with a 90-foot caricature of a suffragette, and the Souvenir Watch Palace was all but overshadowed by a giant, jointed statue of Uncle Sam, reaching one great, hammy hand down into the crowd. "The African Dip" was served up in a refreshment stand shaped like a squatting African. "Creation" turned up again, with the giant naked lady, and a giant replica of some ancient male deity introduced "The Dayton Flood," a variation on "The Galveston Flood" of the St. Louis Fair and "The Johnstown Flood" of the 1901 Buffalo Exposition.[186]

More recent but equally noteworthy examples include the stupendous National Cash Register that toted up daily attendance figures at the portal of the New York World's Fair of 1939; the humanoid facade of Salvador Dali's "Dream of Venus" concession at the same fair, which catapulted the unwary into the Freudian ambiance of a Surrealist nightmare; Cobb's hen-on-eggs-shaped Chicken House eatery at the 1939 San Francisco counterpart to the Flushing Meadow extravaganza (a second overblown cash register loomed nearby); "kiddie-lands" everywhere; the Mitchell, South Dakota, Corn Palace; the Wisconsin Dells; the South Dakota Dinosaur Park in Rapid City – "Childhood Fantasy, Prehistoric Detail" says the free brochure; and any given turning in the path at Disneyland where, with vast mice and ducks dancing in solemn procession, the past of Main Street U.S.A. yields to Fantasyland, Frontierland, Adventureland, and Tomorrowland, under fiercely hygienic conditions.[187]

Dali's Surrealistic "Dream of Venus" attraction at the New York World's Fair, August, 1939. Carl Van Vechten photograph, courtesy of the Museum of the City of New York, New York.

The Wisconsin Dells is a popular resort area alive with colossi advertising rides, tours, souvenirs, and amusements. Photo by Bruce White.

The Dinosaur Park in Rapid City, South Dakota. Photo courtesy of South Dakota Divison of Tourism.

The giant seed and grain murals created annually on the facade of the Corn Palace in Mitchell, South Dakota, a fairyland structure with minarets and odd towers, lends the proper holiday atmosphere to the annual corn festival. Photo courtesy of South Dakota Division of Tourism.

A colossal crowd-pleaser at Walt Disney World in Florida. Photo by Gregory Marling.

NICK CARRAWAY, PAUL BUNYAN, AND BABE, THE BLUE OX
Why Gatsby Is "Great"

Regardless of its particular purpose, the colossus is always a place in itself—a stopping place in time, where the everyday rules of reality are suspended and an idyllic dream commences. Grotesque scale demands a pause—for edification, for commerce, or for the fantastic fun of it. The grotesquerie of fun—the aesthetic of the joke—is a principal and largely neglected ingredient of the midwestern colossus, especially of those roadside sculptures with tangential connections to products and services. The crude Paul Bunyans are fun because their crudity signals a suspension of the rules of sobriety and art. They are overblown, three-dimensional children's drawings. Whereas their size might frighten a child, they stand in the same relationship of scale to the adult as the adult does to the child. Thus the doorway they bid us enter is a time-tunnel back to our own past—not, perhaps, to the world of childhood, but to memories of the delights, security, and illusory bogeymen of a perfect childhood, recalled or imagined.

The grownup child can, for a moment at least, find every dream come true. He can be small and helpless in the face of life and yet trust a big, comforting presence to take care of him. In this world of the imagination, the good guys will always win and Davy Crockett will always prevail. Roadside Bemidji finds its closest analogue in the bum's chorus of "The Big Rock Candy Mountain;" in hobo heaven, "the bulldogs all have rubber teeth and the cops have wooden legs."[188]

The roadside dreamer is a hoaxster, who fools himself on purpose. Taken in conjunction with particular locales, the magical places staked out by the colossi acquire special force in the Midwest. The fun seems more serious there. On the East Coast, in the 1880s and 90s, the colossus ruled the carnival. On the West Coast, in the early 1920s, commerce ruled the colossus. The colossus came to the Midwest in many forms and at many places in the wake of Fitzgerald's meditation on the tragedy of the American frontier, closed forever by Frederick Jackson Turner in 1893, but forcibly wrenched open again in spiritual terms in the pages and images of *The Great Gatsby*.

Fitzgerald did not use the word "great" lightly. Gatsby is a great roadside colossus, an American grotesque, a legendary, storybook hero who stands "for a brief enchanted moment" poised on a pastoral frontier between the expiring East and the unfulfilled promise of a Hollywood West. For Nick, he straddles a frontier as tangible as the soil of Bemidji, Minnesota, and Gatsby gives Nick leave to live out the last, great American dream by slipping back into the national past to find his bearings for the long trip home to the Midwest.

Perhaps Nick drove back west, in the spiffy yellow coupe that doomed Gatsby. It is tempting to imagine that he took old Route 2 toward Bemidji and that, on the outskirts of town, he stopped short and saw, in his mind's eye, two colossal statues, one of Paul Bunyan and the other of Babe, the big Blue Ox. And so he found, at last, that elusive "something commensurate to his capacity for wonder." Inessential reality dimmed and melted. Nick surely laughed away a tear before he pushed on, across that last frontier, and drove away, across the green breast of America, "where the dark fields of the republic rolled on under the night."[189]

A western cowboy dwarfed by Paul and Babe, Bemidji, Minnesota, ca. 1950. Anonymous photograph, from the collections of the Minnesota Historical Society.

Notes

Richard M. Dorson, "Told at the Paul Bunyan Winter Carnival," from *Western Folklore* (1956), quoted in Tristram Potter Coffin and Hennig Cohen, eds., *The Parade of Heroes, Legendary Figures in American Lore* (Garden City, New York: Anchor Press/Doubleday, 1978), p. 603. Dorson cites material gleaned from a United Press article and notes that the same stories, with seasonal flourishes, were trotted out again for press releases heralding the Bemidji Fourth of July Paul Bunyan Festival.

For a lengthy account of the origin and changing meaning of the stories, see Daniel Hoffman, *Paul Bunyan, Last of the Frontier Demigods* (New York: Columbia University Press, 1966), esp. pp. 81-82 on Minnesota festivals. Hoffman and Dorson agree that some manner of "Paul Bunyan's Day" is a crucial feature in the growth of this cycle of myth, and that Bunyan festivals are associated with Minnesota, ca. 1935-1937. Whether Bemidji or Brainerd, Minnesota, was the first town to hold such a festival is still at issue in the scholarly literature. The Bemidji Area Chamber of Commerce, however, issues an information sheet ("The Statues of Paul Bunyan and Babe, the Blue Ox") claiming hegemony for their 1937 celebration. Bemidji, after all, set up permanent statues of the Bunyan characters for their carnival beginning in 1937 (including Paul, Babe, and a giant black duck now installed in the town of Blackduck, Minnesota), whereas Brainerd only acquired a Paul Bunyan colossus in 1950.

John Dos Passos, *Nineteen Nineteen* (New York: Washington Square Press, 1961), pp. 495-96. The novel was originally published by Harcourt Brace in March, 1932.

Carl Sandburg, *The People, Yes* (New York: Harcourt, Brace & Co., 1936), Canto 47, pp. 97-98.

Hoffman, *Paul Bunyan* (1966), pp. 139-42, takes Sandburg to task for deluding "the people" by praising a frontier individualism out of place in modern America. It is, he says, "the ethic of old-style business executives, who, in the assertion of their rights of ownership, leave no ground for intelligent analysis in the solution of economic problems." In Bemidji, Minnesota, however, "intelligent analysis" of what ailed the place economically was not incompatible with a canny espousal of popular mythology.

Joan Shelley Rubin, *Constance Rourke and American Culture* (Chapel Hill: University of North Carolina Press, 1980), pp. 50-53, notes Rourke's early interest in "Paul Bunyon" [sic], expressed in a 1921 article for the *New Republic*.

Harold W. Felton, ed., *Legends of Paul Bunyan* (New York: Alfred A. Knopf, 1947), p. 397, states that "in 1937, the year Paul's statue was completed, it was wired so that he could direct the events during the winter carnival." Citing *Life* Magazine for February 5, 1945 (pp. 58-59), Felton also maintains that the figure of Babe was not completed until 1939.

Timothy J. Garvey, *Popular Monuments of the Midwest: Roadside Colossi as*

Regional Expression, exhibition catalog (Bloomington, Illinois: Illinois Wesleyan University, 1982), unpaginated, and "From *God of Peace* to *Onyx John*: Vulnerability and Change in the Public Monument," unpublished M.A. essay, Department of Art History, University of Minnesota (September, 1978) are pioneering studies of tourist sculpture.

This essay took shape as an address delivered in conjunction with Professor Garvey's Bloomington exhibition, and I am deeply grateful to him for furnishing research slides of older Minnesota sculpture and of more recent colossi manufactured by Creative Display, Inc., of Sparta, Wisconsin.

I am also grateful to the faculty and graduate students of the Department of Geography, the University of Minnesota, for inviting me to share preliminary findings on this subject at their Friday Coffee Hour seminar in March of 1982. The comments of Professor Yi-Fu Tuan were particularly helpful. Further refinements on the theme emerged in a lecture given in the "Critiques 81/82" series at the Cooper Union, New York, in April of 1982, under the auspices of the Humanities Program. Professor Michael Sundell of Cooper Union offered perceptive advice. Finally, the Department of Art History and the American Studies Program at Stanford University gave me the opportunity to submit yet another version of these notions to public scrutiny in May of 1983; Professors Joe and Wanda Corn were gracious hosts and sympathetic critics.

7   Nick Coleman, "Blue Earth puts Golden Spike in Interstate," *Minneapolis Tribune*, September 24, 1978, p. 16A. For the aesthetic of mega-attractions, calculated to divert attention from the modern interstate, as opposed to the older, slower highway, see Michael Albert, "The Transformation of the Roadside Attraction," a paper presented at the annual meeting of the Association of American Geographers, Los Angeles, California, April 20, 1981. Professor Albert, of the University of Wisconsin-River Falls, has been kind enough to share his intriguing ideas with me.

8   Felton, *Legends of Paul Bunyan* (1947), pp. 384-85.

9   *Fact Book, Green Giant Company* (August, 1966), p. 5; *Green Giant Company, Annual Report, Fiscal Year Ending March 31, 1951* (1951), p. 14; *Annual Report, Green Giant Company, Fiscal Year Ended March 31, 1963* (1963), p. 2; and Rick Mitz, "Meet the Little Green Sprout (and how he was created)," *Giant* (March, 1973), pp. 6-9.

10   F. Scott Fitzgerald, *The Great Gatsby* (1925) in Arthur Mizener, ed., *The Fitzgerald Reader* (New York: Charles Scribner's Sons, 1963), pp. 238 and 177.

11   *The Great Gatsby* (1925), p. 238.

12   John Vanderlyn (1801), John Trumbull (1807), and Samuel F. B. Morse (1835) all painted impressive early views of Niagara Falls, for example. Thomas Cole's studies of the high falls of the Genesee River in western New York State reflect this same interest, manifest in the best known of his vista paintings, *The Oxbow (the Connecticut River near Northampton)*, 1836 (The Metropolitan Museum of Art, New York; gift of Mrs. Russell Sage, 1908). The tiny scale of the human figure, the viewer's surrogate in these early wilderness views, is noteworthy.

The "Americanism" of romantic landscape painting of "vast expanse" is suggestively treated in Kynaston McShine, ed., *The Natural Paradise, Painting in America 1800-1950*, exhibition catalog (New York: The Museum of Modern Art, 1976), esp. Robert Rosenblum, "The Primal American Scene," pp. 15-37.

13   Peale's 1801 exhumation of the so-called "Carnivorous Elephant of the North"

is descibed in detail in Charles Coleman Sellers, *Mr. Peale's Museum, Charles Willson Peale and the First Popular Museum of Natural Science and Art* (New York: W. W. Norton & Co./A Barra Foundation Book, 1980), pp. 123-58. Peale's famous self-portrait of 1822 (Pennsylvania Academy of Fine Arts; Joseph and Sarah Harrison Collection) showing the reconstructed mastodon bones is the subject of exhaustive discussion in Roger B. Stein, "Charles Willson Peale's Expressive Design: The Artist in his Museum," *Prospects, The Annual of American Cultural Studies*, 6, Jack Salzman, ed. (New York: Burt Franklin & Co., Inc., 1981), pp. 139-85. In contrast to the small figures shown in the early landscapes, Peale, who beckons the viewer into his domain, dominates the mastodon in scale. Natural science interprets and controls the environment in the fictional world of the painting. Control through human reason and mechanical force is also implicit in Peale's genre portrait of his family overseeing the actual disinterment. See his 1806 *The Exhuming of the Mastodon* (Peale Museum, Baltimore, Maryland; gift of Mrs. Harry White in memory of her husband).

14 Barbara Franco, "The Cardiff Giant: A Hundred Year Old Hoax," *New York History* (October, 1969), pp. 421-40, reprinted as a pamphlet by The New York State Historical Association, Cooperstown, New York (1969). The Cardiff Giant was acquired by the Farmers' Museum, Cooperstown, in 1948.

15 Jane and Michael Stern, *Amazing America* (New York: Random House/David Obst Books, 1978), pp. 93-94. See also David Wallechinsky and Irving Wallace, *The People's Almanac* (Garden City, New York: Doubleday & Co., Inc., 1975), pp. 701-2. Both of these popular texts retain a "gee-whiz" tone suggestive of the Giant's popular reception in 1869.

16 Franco, "The Cardiff Giant" (1969), p. 421, and Curtis D. Macdougall, *Hoaxes* (New York: The Macmillan Company, 1941), pp. 100-102, and Chapter 8, "Incentives to Believe: Chauvinism," pp. 103 ff.

17 Neil Harris, *Humbug, The Art of P. T. Barnum* (Chicago: University of Chicago Press, 1973), pp. 71-72, drawing upon Richard Chase, *Herman Melville: A Critical Study* (1949).

18 Jane Polley, ed., *American Folklore and Legend* (Pleasantville, New York: The Reader's Digest Association, Inc., 1978), p. 144. Again, this text preserves the flavor of wide-eyed wonderment that characterized public response to the tall tale in the 19th century.

19 For pictorial representations from the Crockett Almanacks and a cogent commentary on the growth of American frontier myth, see Joshua C. Taylor, *America As Art* (New York: Harper & Row/Icon Editions, 1976), esp., "The Creation of an American Mythology," pp. 71-94. For Crockett's rivalry with Mike Fink, see Richard M. Dorson, *America in Legend, Folklore from the Colonial Period to the Present* (New York: Random House/Pantheon Books, 1973), pp. 84-85.

20 Versions of the Bunyan story are legion. Among the most interesting retellings during the decades in question is E. R. Jones, *Paul Bunyan—Preface, Prose, Etc.* (privately published, 1930), p. 1, which states that "every Bunyan story is a step into the unknown. It is the triumph of the American engineer over the seemingly impossible. He is always doing the thing that 'can't be done.'" See also James Stevens, *Paul Bunyan* (New York: Alfred A. Knopf, 1925), esp. "The Black Duck Dinner," pp. 104 ff.; Wallace Wadsworth, *Paul Bunyan and*

his Great Blue Ox (Garden City, New York: Doubleday & Company, Inc., 1951), originally published, 1926; and Frank Shay, *Here's Audacity! American Legendary Heroes* (Freeport, New York: Books for Libraries Press, Inc., 1967), originally published, 1930.

21   Karal Ann Marling, *Federal Art in Cleveland, 1933-1943*, exhibition catalog (Cleveland, Ohio: Cleveland Public Library, 1974), p. 38 and Fig. 11. Art created under the new federal patronage programs of the New Deal, beginning in 1933-1934, provides an excellent index of the familiarity and popularity of the new Bunyan legends, since works with arcane themes were not acceptable in programs designed to reach a mass audience. The Bunyan subject was frequently given monumental treatment in both murals and sculpture created in Cleveland; works were pitched at both adult and child audiences.

22   Walter Blair, *Tall Tale America, A Legendary History of Our Humorous Heroes* (New York: Coward-McCann Inc. Publishers, 1944), p. 167. Blair also cites Paul's birth in Maine and the cradle episode, pp. 167-68.

23   Hoffman, *Paul Bunyan* (1966), pp. 81-82, describes this rare, undated pamphlet, published in Minneapolis. He speculates that it was issued in 1935 or 1936; in light of the obvious similarities to events in Bemidji, 1937-1938 seems a more plausible guess. At any rate, the story of Sport is also recounted in detail in W. B. Laughead, *The Marvelous Exploits of Paul Bunyan, As Told in the Camps of the White Pine Lumbermen for Generations* (Minneapolis, Minnesota: The Red River Lumber Company, 1924), 3rd edition, pp. 30-31.

24   Laughead's Brainerd pamphlet is quoted by Hoffman, *Paul Bunyan* (1966), p. 82.

25   Undated publicity release for The Paul Bunyan Amusement Center, Brainerd, Minnesota, available from The Brainerd Baxter Corporation, Brainerd, describes the history of the acquisition. The glowing physical description of the figure comes from the reverse of an old, jumbo color postcard sold in the Brainerd amusement park and issued by Northern Minnesota Novelties, Crosslake, Minnesota. The card took a 3-cent stamp.

26   Postcard text; see note 25, above. Copyrighted postcards being issued today by the same firm feature an edited version of the description. The dimensions and clothing sizes are still cited, but gone are the extravagant claims that this is "the largest animated man in the world," and "a true mechanical figure of the legendary Minnesota's Paul Bunyan." The change hints at a diminution in the hostilities between Brainerd and Bemidji.

Northern Minnesota Novelties' (now NMN, Inc.) postcard text for its views of the Paul and Babe in Bemidji has not changed, although the photograph of the sculpture has: "These huge figures of steel and concrete built on the shore of Lake Bemidji are emblematical of the days of the early lumberjack who originated lumbercamp whoppers of Paul & Babe that have been handed down for generations. These stories, never heard outside the haunts of the lumberjack until recent years, are declared by some literary authorities to be 'the only true American myth.' "

27   These sculptural sequels are later in date but are stylistically close to the Bemidji figures in shape, finish, color, and intention. The Brainerd figure, purchased by local entrepreneurs and installed in its present location in 1949-1950, has a two-dimensional Babe painted on the back wall of the enclosure that covers the statue. The sculptural Babe now in the parking lot

of the Paul Bunyan Center (an amusement park) was added at a later date. According to the NMN postcard of Babe, it was "constructed in Kansas City, Mo. by Joe T. Bowen. Shipped in one piece by railroad flatcar over five railroads. Weight 3600 pounds, height 15 feet, length 23 feet, width between horn tips 10 feet."

When I visited the Bemidji Area Chamber of Commerce information center at 3rd and Bemidji Avenue in the summer of 1983, the giant Bunyan artifacts on exhibit included the following: toothbrush, undershorts, candle with holder, telephone, fish line and hook, blotter, walking stick, axe, playing cards, dice, toothpaste, belt, fingernail clippings, billfold and money, comb, toothpick, rifle, watch, belt buckle (a horseshoe!), razor, potato masher, penny, ring, cigar, chocolate bar, cowbell (for Lucy, the cow who ate whole evergreen trees and thus gave pungent milk used for cough medicine and liniment), landing net, and one, lone giant green bean. The grounds of the Paul Bunyan Center in Brainerd are also littered with accessories. In addition to Sport, "the inside-out dog," there are Henry the Squirrel, a mailbox, telephone, grindstone, fishing pole, ice cream cone, beer mug, axe, wishing well, and an assortment of giant daffodils, serving as street lights, and mushrooms, sheltering picnic tables.

The Hackensack piece was fabricated locally in 1954. It stands on the shore of Birch Lake, on a lot also occupied by the log cabin headquarters of the Chamber of Commerce, in whose custody Lucette remains. Constructed of a plasterlike material applied over a wire mesh armature, the statue is hollow and the interior accessible through a wooden port hidden in the lakefront side of her wind-tossed skirt. A hand-lettered signboard at the base of the statue reads: "Hackensack [,] Home of Paul Bunyan's Sweetheart [,] LucetteDiana Kensack." On July 2, 1983, the statue was tacky to the touch and the grass around it littered with flakes of last season's skin; it is apparent that the appearance of the statue is deemed important to the local tourist industry.

The Paul Bunyan cradle in Akeley is a wooden, homemade affair, tucked away in a little roofed shelter near the town bandstand. The tourist taking the trouble to find the monument is rewarded with Minnesota's only accurate account of the genesis of Paul Bunyan:

> In the early 19 hundreds the Red River Lumber Company Mill, located here in Akeley, Minnesota, printed the first stories about Paul Bunyan and his Blue Ox. Hence, Akeley is the true birthplace of Paul Bunyan.
>
> This large cradle signifies Akeley as being the birthplace of Paul Bunyan.

Akeley was Paul Bunyan's birthplace, and Minnesota his playground. The Bunyan boat anchor in Ortonville was erected in 1958 as a part of the Minnesota Centennial celebration, and is graced with a plaque signed by then-Governor Orville Freeman, explaining Paul's hitherto unchronicled activities as a sports fisherman. The text also notes the cooperation of the local granite industry. The anchor is, in fact, a massive, rectangular slab of local granite raised into the air on four stubby stone legs that afford just enough room to insert a wayside picnic table beneath. One identifies the slab as an anchor only because of a hooklike arrangement of stiffened chain-links (often used as whimsical supports for rural mailboxes in the Midwest) protruding from the top. Situated at a roadside overlook above Big Stone Lake, this ungainly monument, like the others in the Bunyan group, exists to promote trade and tourism.

"Paul's Giant Black Duck" in Blackduck, Minnesota, was made in Bemidji for the Winter Carnival of 1937; see note 1, above. And it has fallen on evil times. The white picket fence that used to mark the site as special has disappeared, and the duck itself is in need of cosmetic work. The paint is worn off in patches and the concrete fabric of the statue is also corroded. A newer, more attractive, and better-maintained Black Duck about half as large as the civic prototype stands outside the Drake Motel, on Route 71, at the edge of town. Thus, in October of 1983, the town wisely purchased a new fiberglass duck from F.A.S.T. of Wisconsin.

The Kelliher gravesite is a splendidly inventive colossus, albeit one exceedingly difficult to spot unless word of its existence reaches the tourist in advance. I visited the burial mound in the middle of a howling thunderstorm, and the gigantic fury of the wind was enough to convince anyone that giant men once roamed the area. The grave is located in a little park that provides campsites and tourist facilities; rather than a lure for passing motorists, the Kelliher colossus seems to be a kind of mental souvenir—something a visitor stumbles across and never forgets.

Nonetheless, this Minnesota family of Bunyan sculptures as a whole does suggest an analogy with what J. B. Jackson called "other directed architecture," designed to attract and to profit from the passerby; see J. B. Jackson, "Other Directed Houses," in Erwin H. Zube, ed., *Landscapes: Selected Writings of J. B. Jackson* (Amherst: University of Massachusetts Press, 1970), pp. 55-72.

See also Dean MacCannell, *The Tourist, A New Theory of the Leisure Class* (New York: Schocken Books, 1976).

28   Tristram Potter Coffin and Hennig Cohen, eds., *The Parade of Heroes, Legendary Figures in American Lore* (Garden City, New York: Anchor Press/Doubleday, 1978), pp. 487-93, includes the 1910 story by MacGillivray from the *Detroit News Tribune* and testimony from Laughead, who began publishing Bunyan stories in the trade journal ads of the Red River Lumber Company in 1914. This ad campaign culminated in the 1922 promotional booklet entitled *Paul Bunyan and His Big Blue Ox*, the titular theme of the Bemidji sculptural group. According to Coffin and Cohen, the Paul Bunyan Winter Carnival in Bemidji became a major source of fresh Bunyan material in its own right, as old-timers huddled together in the back rooms of local stores and told yarns to distract themselves from temperatures regularly plummeting to 30 below. It was under such conditions that the colorful Bunyan ensemble was expected to lure tourists to a carnival week, during which winter sports enthusiasts stayed outside in the cold and rivaled the hero's feats of physical prowess. One such story had it that Bunyan lit a fire under the local lake and tossed in some vegetables to make pea soup for his logging crew; then he carried a paddle-wheel steamer north from New Orleans to cruise the lake and so to stir the soup.

See also P. M. Clepper, "The Real, Unvarnished, Unexpected, Hitherto Suppressed, Almost-Never-Before-Revealed Secret Truth About Paul Bunyan," *Northliner Magazine*, 3, #1 (Winter, 1972), pp. 12-13, 17.

The role of the Minneapolis ad man in creating the Bunyan character is, of course, flatly denied in other parts of the nation with a stake in the legend. Acknowledging that "even today, Minnesota or Michigan claims he was a native son," Bangor, Maine, stoutly insists that "Paul Bunyan was born in Bangor on Feb. 12, 1834, by coincidence the day the Queen City was incorporated. A mammoth, 31-foot statue of Paul stands near the municipal auditorium as a reminder of his origins;" "Paul Bunyan, Legendary Woodsman, Was Born in Bangor," *Inflight Magazine*, 2, #2 (March-April, 1982), unpaginated. This Bunyan statue, and another once situated in downtown Portland, Maine, is among a handful of such civic pieces located outside the Midwest.

Laughead, *Marvelous Exploits* (1924), p. 3.   29

Hoffman, *Paul Bunyan* (1966), p. 82. See also Richard M. Dorson, *American*   30
Folklore (Chicago: University of Chicago Press, 1977), pp. 199-200, for Bunyan
as a resort promoter's dream, a "mass-culture hero." Dorson, p. 224, also
discusses the Brainerd and Bemidji festivals, and notes that from there,
such community galas spread to Concord, New Hampshire, and Tacoma,
Washington: "Sometimes images of Paul are fashioned from snow or
metal or men of heroic proportions play Bunyan for the day. So fast and far
had the 'myth' spiralled upward into the popular imagination that figures of
Old Paul adorned both the New York and the California World's Fairs of
1939."

Sinclair Lewis, *Babbitt* (New York: New American Library, 1961), pp. 32-33.   31
The novel was originally published by Harcourt, Brace & World, Inc., in 1922.
The Minnesota locales in Lewis's novels are analyzed by John J. Koblas,
Sinclair Lewis, Home At Last (Bloomington, Minnesota: Voyageur Press,
1981). See esp. pp. 47-49, for a piece of doggerel attributing the gargantuan
appetites of the deceased Paul Bunyan to several of the author's Minnesota
friends. Lewis, who spent some time in a lumber camp in Cass Lake, Minne-
sota, in 1918 (his collection of pseudo-folkloric lyrics, *Ballads and Songs of the*
Shanty-Boy, 1926, reflects the experience), associated Paul Bunyan with
Bemidji in the only verse of the poem to mention a specific locale:

> From Ball Club to Bemidji folks
> Would hide beneath their beds
> When they saw John and Robert roll
> Off drunken from their sleds.

Lewis, *Babbitt* (1922), pp. 33 and 124.   32

For tourism and motoring in the Depression, see "The Great American   33
Roadside," *Fortune*, 10, #3 (September, 1934), pp. 53-63, 172, 174, and 177,
with illustrations by John Steuart Curry. The double-page map of tourist attractions shows absolutely nothing in the Upper Midwest, along Routes 2 and
10. The map is blank from Lake Superior to the Black Hills, where the legend
notes that "Here Borglum is chiselling on Mt. Rushmore a monument seven
and one half times the size of the Sphinx."

For the Beadle novels and the cultural resonance of the frontier myth in   34
general, see Henry Nash Smith, *Virgin Land, The American West in Symbol and*
Myth (Cambridge, Mass.: Harvard University Press, 1970), esp. pp. 90-111.

For the appeal of Barnum's elephants, his oddities, and the "colossal giants"   35
he routinely touted "whenever he had no stupendous exhibition to offer," see
Susan Estabrook Kennedy, "The Public's Obedient Servant, P. T. Barnum,"
Prospects, An Annual of American Cultural Studies, 4, Jack Salzman, ed. (New
York: Burt Franklin & Co., Inc., 1979), esp. pp. 314-15. Lewis A. Erenberg,
Steppin' Out, New York Nightlife and the Transformation of American Culture,
1890-1930 (Westport, Connecticut: Greenwood Press, 1981), p. 16, provides a
sound analysis of the rural, frontier aspect of circus entertainment. He suggests
that the imaginative self-identification of the urban audience with the derring-
do of the animal trainer subduing the monster is crucial. The Victorian circus
is thus a cultural metaphor for the subjugation of "the wildness of life and
brought order and high civilization in its wake." Erenberg concentrates on the
issue of entertainment as a mechanism of control, but one might as readily note
its function as a temporal interregnum, a special occasion for acting out com-

pelling and haunting fantasies. Applying the same reasoning to Wild West shows and stories, the audience vicariously tames anarchic nature at a frontier delimited by the temporal act of watching or reading. Inasmuch as a suspension of orderly, sequential "monochronic" time is one of the principal aesthetic demands made by the spatial characteristics of the roadside colossus, the act of viewing the colossus might be said to occur in and to create "polychronic" time; see Edward T. Hall, *The Hidden Dimension* (Garden City, New York: Anchor Press/Doubleday, 1969), esp. p. 173.

It is in this sense, it would appear, that Erenberg sees the electrified, nighttime dazzle of the Broadway entertainment district in Gatsby's era as a new human frontier of joy and fun, a magical zone that, once traversed, liberates the cafe-goer from everyday rules, routine, and social authority; p. 118.

36   Barbara Novak, *Nature and Culture, American Landscape and Painting, 1825-1875* (New York: Oxford University Press, 1980), p. 145. See also Frank Bergon and Zeese Papanikolas, eds., introduction to *Looking Far West: The Search for the American West in History, Myth, and Literature* (New York: New American Library, 1978), p. 8.

37   Peter Hassrick, *The Way West, Art Of Frontier America* (New York: Harry N. Abrams, Inc., 1977), pp. 120-29. The painting, *Domes of the Yosemite*, 1867, measures 9′8″ x 15′, and is in the collection of the St. Johnsbury Athenaeum, Inc., St. Johnsbury, Vermont.

38   Carol Clark, *Thomas Moran, Watercolors of the American West* (Austin, Texas: University of Texas Press/Amon Carter Museum of Western Art, 1980), p. 47.

39   For the genesis and rejection of *The Last of the Buffalo*, see Gordon Hendricks, *Albert Bierstadt: Painter of the American West* (New York: Harry N. Abrams, 286 ff. The painting is now in the Corcoran Gallery of Art collection, Washington, D.C. (gift of Mrs. Albert Bierstadt). A smaller version is in the Buffalo Bill Historical Center collection, Cody, Wyoming.

40   Walt Whitman, *Specimen Days* (Boston: David R. Godine, 1971), p. 94. The book was first published in 1882. For Whitman's attitudes toward landscape, see Novak, *Nature and Culture* (1980), pp. 153-56.

41   Halsey C. Ives, intro., *The Dream City, a Portfolio of Photographic Views of the World's Columbian Exposition* (St. Louis, Missouri: N. D. Thompson Publishing Company, 1893), unpaginated plate caption, entitled "Arab Spearmen of the Wild East Show."

42   Don Russell, "Wild West show," in Howard R. Lamar, ed., *The Reader's Encyclopedia of the American West* (New York: Thomas Y. Crowell Company, 1977), pp. 1269-70.

43   Ives, *The Dream City* (1893), unpaginated plate caption, "Hunter's Cabin."

44   For the metaphorical content of Bierstadt's painting, see Dawn Glanz, *How the West Was Drawn, American Art and the Settling of the Frontier* (Ann Arbor, Michigan: UMI Research Press, 1982), pp. 106-8.

45   Ives, *The Dream City* (1893), unpaginated plate captions, entitled "The Moose Bridge" and "The Farmers' Bridge."

46   See, for example, John Whitman, *The Best Free Attractions in the Midwestern States* (Deephaven, Minnesota: Meadowbrook Press, 1981), p. 101, and Stern,

Amazing America (1978), p. 312. David A. Dary, *The Buffalo Book, The Saga of an American Symbol* (New York: Avon Books/ A Discus Book, 1975), unpaginated plate section following p. 282 realizes that the buffalo is a monument and cites its vital statistics: "Made of 8″ steel H beams, rods, wire mesh, concrete, stucco; 26′ high, 46′ long, 60 tons wgt. Sculptor, Elmer Peterson." The North Dakota Travel Division and a promotional booklet distributed by Frontier Village concur, adding that this work of "artistic genius" eventually cost $11,000 to complete.

Ives, *The Dream City* (1893), unpaginated plate captions, entitled "Proctor's Cowboy" and "Proctor's Indian." See also *Photo-Gravures of the World's Columbian Exposition* (Chicago: A. Wittemann, 1893), unpaginated.   47

Ives, *The Dream City* (1893), unpaginated plate caption, entitled "The Heroic Statue of the Republic."   48

"A Mid-Western Sculptor, the Art of Lorado Taft," *The Mentor*, 11, #9 (October, 1923), pp. 19-34. Taft first came to national attention with several sculptural groups on the Horticulture Building at the Columbian Exposition. Thereafter, he devoted the greater part of his career to redesigning what had been the Fair's Midway Plaisance as an integral part of the Chicago park system through the placement of colossal fountains of his own devising. The *Fountain of Time* was to stand at the west end of the axis, facing the *Fountain of Creation (Evolution)*. Between the two, as monumental crossings over a formal canal, he planned a *Bridge of the Sciences*, *Bridge of the Arts*, and *Bridge of Religions*. For his thoughts on the work of French, Potter, and his other senior colleagues at the Fair, see Lorado Taft, *The History of American Sculpture* (New York: The Macmillan Company, 1917), pp. 474-75 ff.   49

Lorado Taft, "The Joyous Adventure of Bringing Art to the People," taken from an address delivered in 1928 and appended to Ruth Helming Mose, "Midway Studios," *American Magazine of Art*, 19, #8 (August, 1928), p. 423.   50

Wallace Heckman, *Lorado Taft's Indian Statue, "Black Hawk," An Account of the Unveiling Ceremonies at Eagle's Nest Bluff, Oregon, Illinois, July the First, Nineteen Hundred and Eleven, Frank O. Lowden Presiding* (Chicago: University of Chicago Press, 1912), p. 16.   51

Hamlin Garland, "The Trail Markers," in Heckman, *Unveiling Ceremonies* (1912), p. 91. This is the concluding stanza.   52

Lorado Taft, quoted in Heckman, *Unveiling Ceremonies* (1912), pp. 95-97. See also J. C. Chandler, "Eagle's Nest Camp; Barbizon of Chicago Artists," *Art and Archaeology*, 12 (November, 1921), pp. 194-204. According to Chandler, the art of most of the colonists became affected by the Indian motif.   53

I am grateful to my friend Professor James Dennis, Department of Art History, University of Wisconsin – Madison, for calling *Black Hawk* to my attention in the first place, and for noting that the fame of the work hinged, in part at any rate, on the use of reinforced concrete. See also Marion E. Gridley, *America's Indian Statues* (Chicago: Towerton Press/The Amerindian, 1966), p. 4.

The Greatest of Expositions, Completely Illustrated (St. Louis, Missouri: Official Photographic Company of the Louisiana Purchase Exposition, 1904), p. 143, and Margaret Johanson Witherspoon, *Remembering the St. Louis World's Fair* (St. Louis, Missouri: Eden Publishing House, 1973), map, pp. 88-9. See also Peter H. Hassrick, *Frederic Remington* (New York: Harry N. Abrams/New   54

American Library, 1975), unpaginated caption accompanying Plate 57, noting that a second plaster replica was set up at the main entrance to the 1905 Lewis and Clark Exposition in Portland, Oregon, an altogether more amusement-mad fair than that in St. Louis.

55   For examples of his articles, see Peggy and Harold Samuels, eds., *The Collected Writings of Frederic Remington* (Garden City, New York: Doubleday & Company, 1979).

56   Burton Benedict, M. Miriam Dobkin, and Elizabeth Armstrong, *A Catalogue of Posters, Photographs, Paintings, Drawings, Furniture, Documents, Souvenirs, Statues, Books, Medals, Dolls, Music Sheets, Postcards, Curiosities, Banners, Awards, Remains, Etcetera from San Francisco's Panama Pacific International Exposition, 1915,* exhibition catalog (Berkeley, California: The Lowie Museum of Anthropology, University of California, Berkeley, 1982), unpaginated text accompanying entry A3. For *End of the Trail,* see entry D87. I am grateful to my friend Professor Sheila ffolliott of George Mason University, Fairfax, Virginia, for alerting me to the importance of the San Francisco Fair and for insisting that I attend Berkeley's fine show.

See also Elizabeth N. Armstrong, "Hercules and the Muses: Public Art at the Fair," pp. 120-23 in Burton Benedict, *The Anthropology of World's Fairs, San Francisco's Panama Pacific International Exposition of 1915* (Berkeley, California: The Lowie Museum of Anthropology/Scolar Press, 1983).

57   Martin H. Bush, *James Earle Fraser: American Sculptor,* exhibition catalog (New York: Kennedy Galleries, Inc., 1969), pp. 5 and 16, and J. Walker McSpadden, *Famous Sculptors of America* (New York: Dodd, Mead & Company, 1924), pp. 281-82.

58   Aline B. Louchheim, "Most Famous Unknown Sculptor," *New York Times Magazine,* 100 (May 13, 1951), p. 24.

59   See *Official Publication, Panama Pacific International Exposition, San Francisco 1915, Hand-Colored* (San Francisco: The Hibernia Bank, 1982[?]), an unpaginated reproduction of one such "official" souvenir album.

60   Louchheim, "Most Famous Unknown Sculptor" (1951), p. 66. This same figure is cited by Fraser himself, quoted in McSpadden, *Famous Sculptors* (1924), p. 281.

61   "James Earle Fraser Dies," *New York Times* (October 12, 1953), p. 27. See also Bush, *James Earle Fraser* (1969), p. 16.

62   Quoted by McSpadden, *Famous Sculptors* (1924), p. 282. In 1927 Fraser was indeed chosen to make a heroic-sized Lincoln for the beginning of the transcontinental Lincoln Highway in Jersey City, New Jersey.

The Visalia piece is now in the collection of the Cowboy Hall of Fame, Oklahoma City, Oklahoma. A smaller cast, in bronze, was unveiled in 1929 at Shaler Park, Waupan, Wisconsin.

63   Quoted by McSpadden, *Famous Sculptors* (1924), p. 281.

64   For a discussion of the Colossus of Rhodes in a modern and specifically American context, see Marvin Trachtenberg, *The Statue of Liberty* (London: Penguin Books, Ltd., 1976), esp. pp. 112-13 and 117. Trachtenberg stresses the aesthetic function of the great statue at Rhodes—one of Antipater's Seven

Wonders of the ancient world—as an "emblematic facade" for the seaport and hence a prototype for F. A. Bartholdi's Statue of Liberty in New York harbor. The Statue of Liberty serves as a facade or ceremonial gateway for the American nation and land mass.

In both literary tradition and in reconstructions (for example, Fisher von Erlach's 1712 engraving), the lost Colossus at Rhodes was also a "pharos," or lighthouse, a structure defining a border between nautical and terrestrial orders of experience, outside and inside, journey and destination, and so on. As a lighthouse, the Colossus of Rhodes carried a vessel of fire in its upraised right arm. In New York's torch-bearing Statue of Liberty, the Rhodian tradition is thus readily conflated with the lost Pharos of Alexandria, another of the canonical ancient wonders, which, Trachtenberg argues, inspired Richard Morris Hunt's design for the base supporting the Bartholdi statue.

Later funerary usages inspired by the ancient Sphinx at Giza are considered by James Stevens Curl, *A Celebration of Death* (New York: Charles Scribner's Sons, 1980), pp. 9-10, 194-95 and *passim*. Edmund Gillan, Jr., *Victorian Cemetery Art* (New York: Dover Publications, Inc., 1972), plates 63, 193, and 197, illustrates several 19th-century American sphinxes in New York and Massachusetts. In addition to their function as lion-guardians of the portals of death, at least one of these domestic examples—that in Mt. Auburn Cemetery, Cambridge, Massachusetts—seems to have specific geographic connotations. This sphinx was erected by local abolitionists to honor freed slaves and so identifies the African continent as the freedmen's point of origin. Thus the monument gestures backward, into the historical past of the deceased, and forward into the realm of the hereafter. It is a decisive facade or portal, dividing orders of time, space, and human experience, and bringing them into play at a specified place—the monument—which becomes the stage for ritualistic passage between these alternative states.

65   Professor John Modell, Carnegie-Mellon University, has suggested that the concept of liminality is germane to an understanding of Paul Bunyan and his sculptural kinfolk, all the more so in that the midwestern roadside colossus occupies the realm of leisure, or purposeful play. Thus the application of Victor Turner's study of ritual process in Roland A. Delattre, "The Rituals of Humanity and the Rhythms of Reality," *Prospects, An Annual of American Cultural Studies*, 5, Jack Salzman, ed. (New York: Burt Franklin & Co., Inc., 1980), esp. pp. 42-43, has been crucial to the formulation of my thesis that the colossus gives concrete ceremonial and spatial focus to a ritual process. As object and occasion—space, place, and time—the colossus answers Delattre's definition of the capacity of ritual "to tap a variety of energies and to clear channels of significance through which they may flow." The colossus is a figurative "clear channel," or, in literal terms, a gateway, a sluice. The kind of internal drama reified and activated at this gateway, insofar as it relates to the world of advertising and to the "everyday life" of leisure and tourism, is discussed in Raymond Williams, *Drama in a Dramatised Society* (Cambridge: Cambridge University Press, 1975), esp. p. 5 ff.

66   Pliny is quoted by Virginia Bush, *The Colossal Sculpture of the Cinquecento* (New York: Garland Publishing, Inc., 1976), pp. xxv-xxvi, who also summarizes the subsequent history of the term.

67   It is worth noting that the only post-Renaissance monograph on colossi was E. Lesbazeilles' *Les colosses anciens et modernes* of 1881, a study made with and for his friend Bartholdi, of Statue of Liberty fame. See Ruth McKenney and

Eileen Bransten, "The Colossus," *New York* [*New York Herald Tribune*] (October 24, 1965), p. 15 ff.

For the wicker-work parade giants of medieval England, see John Michell, *The Earth Spirit, Its Ways, Shrines and Mysteries* (New York: Crossroad Publishing Co., 1975), unpaginated Plate 32.

68   Bush, *Colossal Sculpture* (1976), pp. 11, 88-92.

69   For the colossi known in Rome during the Renaissance, see Francis Haskell and Nicholas Penny, *Taste and the Antique, The Lure of Classical Sculpture, 1500-1900* (New Haven, Connecticut: Yale University Press, 1982), pp. 258-59, 272-73, and *passim.*

70   *The Great Gatsby* (1925), p. 121. Paul Fussell, *The Great War and Modern Memory* (New York: Oxford University Press, 1977), p. 23, barely hints that Fitzgerald's "valley of ashes" and by extension, the tenor of the novel as a whole, depend on the rhetoric of World War I and the physical, psychic, and historical frontier of the trenches. His extended disquisition on the application of "Myth, Ritual, and Romance," pp. 139-42, to the literary formulation of the trench experience, which, in turn, shaped post-war literary typology, is directly applicable, in detail, to the industrial/pastoral imagery of *The Great Gatsby,* however. So is his argument for the centrality of John Bunyan's *Pilgrim's Progress* and the Biblical "Valley of the Shadow of Death" to wartime chronicles and post-war fiction. My own reading of the role of ritual places and their monuments in 1920s and 30s America provides artifactual support for Fussell's provocative hypothesis.

71   *The Great Gatsby* (1925), p. 121.

72   On fads, see Nunally Johnson, "Here We Go A-Nutting!" *Saturday Evening Post,* 203, #13 (September 27, 1930), pp. 13 and 110. The article dubs miniature golf a fad, along with flagpole sitting and various feats of eating.

73   Frederick Lewis Allen, *Since Yesterday, The Nineteen-Thirties in America* (New York: Bantam Books, 1965), pp. 15 and 26-27.

74   Elmer Davis, "Miniature Golf to the Rescue," *Harper's Magazine,* 162 (December, 1930), pp. 5-6.

75   *Miniature Golf, A Treatise on the Subject Containing Business Building Ideas* (Denver, Colorado: Central States Publishing Company, 1930), pp. 17 and 57.

76   "Tom Thumb Golf," *The Nation,* 131, #3399 (August 27, 1930), pp. 215-16.

77   *Miniature Golf* (1930), pp. 20 and 52.

78   John Held, Jr., "The Holy Bonds," in *The Flesh is Weak* (New York: The Vanguard Press, 1931), pp. 27-28.

79   Held, *The Flesh is Weak* (1931), p. 26.

80   Davis, "Miniature Golf to the Rescue" (1930), p. 4 ff.

81   "Bobby Jones of the Vacant-Lot Golf Clubs," *Literary Digest,* 106, #8 (August 23, 1930), pp. 32-34. See also "Golf at the Fireside," *Literary Digest,* 108, #2 (January 10, 1931), p. 35.

82   "Miniature Golf Helps Many Kinds of Business," *Business Week,* 5 (September 3, 1930), pp. 9-10.

Allen, *Since Yesterday* (1965), p. 26, and *Business Week* (1930), p. 9 cite the same figures.

83

Michael J. Phillips, *How to Play Miniature Golf, A Complete and Correct Description of the Art of the Newest Sport* (Los Angeles, California: Keystone Publishing Company, 1930), pp. 10 and 12. Phillips was also the editor of a bimonthly magazine, *Miniature Golf Player*, advertised on the flyleaf of the book. At $2 per annum, it was described thus: "Lots of pictures; gossipy; snappily written. Makes you yearn to grab that ol' putter and go to it."

84

Phillips, *How to Play* (1930), p. 12. Tom Thumb Golf was Carter's patented product, distributed by the Fairyland Mfg. Co. as a way of marketing cotton-seed hulls; it was bought out by National Pipe Products Corp. Another patented system was called Bob-O-Link.

85

Mara Evans, "Lilliput Putters," *Saturday Evening Post*, 203, #13 (September 27, 1930), p. 13. My colleague, Professor Rob Silberman, has suggested to me that billiards and miniature golf have a great deal in common. Alfred Stieglitz, he notes, was a billiards fanatic who became a miniature golf addict after a course opened near his summer home at Lake George, New York.

86

Phillips, *How to Play* (1930), p. 53.

87

See the International Newsreel Photo in "Bobby Jones of the Vacant-Lot Golf Clubs," *Literary Digest* (1930), p. 32.

88

Phillips, *How to Play* (1930), p. 39. "Even Crazier Hazards of the Tom Thumb Links," *Literary Digest*, 108, #4 (January 24, 1931), p. 37, reports on the state of the art in London, where a monkey hazard entailed shooting the ball through the animal's cage without having it "lifted" and a metal sea-serpent hazard, wound around a tree, that swallowed the ball and shot it out again, in a different direction, via the tail. There was also something called a "howitzer hole" involving toy cannons and trenches full of tin soldiers.

89

Nathaniel West, *The Day of the Locust* (New York: Bantam Books, 1975), p. 3. The novel was originally published in 1939.

90

West, *Day of the Locust* (1939), p. 13.

91

The image recalls the dead Gatsby, floating in his own pool. In this detail, as in many others—most obviously, the extended parody of the "valley of ashes" scene in the description of the studio's set dump—*The Day of the Locust* is the tragicomic, western postscript to *The Great Gatsby*.

92

Sinclair Lewis, *The Man Who Knew Coolidge, Being the Soul of Lowell Schmaltz, Constructive and Nordic Citizen* (New York: Harcourt, Brace and Company, 1928), p. 234.

93

"The Great American Roadside," *Fortune*, 10, #3 (September, 1934), pp. 53 and 57.

94

"The Great American Roadside," *Fortune* (1934), p. 60.

95

See "The Great American Roadside," *Fortune* (1934), p. 172, for a Keystone Photo of "Freda Farms," an ice-cream-bucket-shaped ice cream stand outside Hartford, Connecticut.

96

For a concise history of shop signs and cigarstore Indians, see Tom Armstrong, "The Innocent Eye, American Folk Sculpture," in *200 Years of American*

97

Sculpture, exhibition catalog (New York: Whitney Museum of American Art/ David R. Godine, 1976), pp. 75-111. The temporal relationship between a revival of interest in folk and popular advertising sculpture, Dr. Eckleburg's eyes, and the Bemidji group is telling. The revival began in 1924 with a major exhibition "Early American Art," at the Whitney Studio Club, forerunner of the Whitney Museum of American Art. For an account of that revival, see Beatrix T. Rumford, "Uncommon Art of the Common People: A Review of Trends in the Collecting and Exhibiting of American Folk Art," in Ian M. G. Quimby and Scott T. Swank, eds., *Perspectives on American Folk Art* (Winterthur, Delaware: Winterthur Museum/W. W. Norton & Co., 1980), pp. 13-53.

Holger Cahill, whose curatorial work at the Newark Museum stimulated interest, became director of the Federal Art Project of the Works Progress Administration in 1935. The WPA's Index of American Design, established under Cahill's guidance in the spring of 1935, set unemployed artists to work making accurate and highly detailed renderings of the national heritage of "people's" or popular artifacts. Sculptural figureheads, weathervanes, hitching posts, circus and carrousel figures, cigarstore Indians, and shop signs were singled out for special treatment. Clarence P. Hornung, *Treasury of American Design, A Pictorial Survey of Popular Folk Arts Based upon Watercolor Renderings in the Index of American Design, at the National Gallery of Art* (New York: Harry N. Abrams, Inc., 1976), Vol. 1, p. 83, plate 261, reproduces an Index rendering of Eckleburg's eyes—huge, blue, and framed by yellow spectacles—under the caption, "Sign with spectacles and eyes, designating an optician's shop, c. 1875." It is self-evident, therefore, that Fitzgerald's sign was based on a real prototype and that reference to such signs was a topical, even fashionable, allusion in 1925.

Gigantic chickens, plowboys, and cones, along with huge fish, cows, steers, and ears of corn, are among the products routinely manufactured and sold by Creative Display, Inc., F.A.S.T. Corp. (Fantastic Animals, Shapes & Trademarks), Sculptured Advertising, Inc., and a handful of rival firms in the Midwest of the present day. Garvey, *Popular Monuments* (1982), unpaginated, argues that in addition to promoting products and services, these familiar, hulking landmarks of the Midwest, perfect in their symmetry and surface gloss, "promote an . . . exaggerated picture of the virtues of the region. Where going-to-market weight is the primary measure of value, statues of . . . herefords twenty-one feet long or three hundred pound ears of corn represent true ideals . . . and operating within the region containing such overwhelming natural riches is an army of giants, . . . *Big Boys* tall enough to stand as beacons directing lost freeway drivers into the safe haven of interstate restaurants." The popular, mass-produced colossi of the Midwest are, therefore, "not only the largest, but the best and the brightest."

Creative Display and rival firms also manufacture floats. Stationary roadside figures are clearly related to the motor-driven parade float, which also rose to cultural prominence for the first time in the 1930s, displacing mummers, musicians, and other costumed performers. As an example, the town of Rockport, Massachusetts, mounted on a truckbed an almost life-sized replica of the fishhouse pier often depicted by its resident artists' colony, and sent it to the American Legion Chicago Convention parade, held in tandem with the Century of Progress Exposition in 1933. The float took first prize in the competition; see John L. Cooley, *Rockport Sketch Book* (Rockport, Massachusetts: Rockport Art Association, 1965), p. 105.

Sally Henderson and Robert Landau, *Billboard Art* (San Francisco: Chronicle

Books, 1981), pp. 10-13, point out that under fiercely competitive urban conditions in the 19th century, some merchants commissioned hugely oversized samples of their wares—hats, shoes, and the like—set them on wheels, and had them paraded through the streets. The outsized shoe was still a feature of window displays, especially in men's shoe stores, in the 1950s and 60s.

The range and number of roadside colossi in Minnesota are astounding. In addition to the pieces mentioned, there are numerous wholly commercial figures, such as the Indian at Bloomington, the polar bear at White Bear Lake, a clutch of "Happy Chefs," and a whole school of giant fishes adorning the several branches of Morey's Fish House. The 102-foot "Hermann the German" at New Ulm—a statue of Hermann the Cheruscan, a Germanic hero who defeated the Romans in 9 A.D.—was conceived in deadly earnest. See Michell, *The Earth Spirit* (1975), unpaginated Plate 44 for Hermann's prototype, a colossal statue of Arminius in the Teutoburger Wald. Derham Groves, a student in Landscape Architecture at the University of Minnesota, now completing a study of the Hermann monument, suggests that New Ulm German-Americans were aware of the frontier implications of their colossus. It was, in fact, meant to commemorate their resistance to the Indian uprisings of the late 19th century. **98**

By contrast, "Big Ole," the 28-foot, locally produced centerpiece of the resort town of Alexandria, is more lighthearted. He bears the legend, "Alexandria, Birthplace of America," emblazoned on his shield and this big Viking stands as the community's seriocomic act of faith in the authenticity of the dubious Kensington Runestone (plaster paperweight reproductions of both "Big Ole" and the runestone are sold in the "museum" and tourist information center just behind the statue), used by natives as proof that the Viking ancestors of the modern Scandinavian-Americans of the area settled America before Columbus arrived and settled first in western Minnesota. "Big Ole" was once mobile, traveling for exhibition purposes to the 1964 New York World's Fair, although the statue is too large and cumbersome to be classified as a traditional float.

Because colossal sculpture is not only endemic to the Midwest but widely regarded by residents as emblematic of their region, it is frequently dislodged and shipped off to national fairs and expositions. "Chatty Belle," a 20-foot-tall statue billed as "the largest talking cow in the world" made an appearance in the Wisconsin Pavilion at the 1964 New York World's Fair. Normally Belle and her baby, "Bullet," are roadside attractions in Neillsville, Wisconsin, a cheese center.

In addition to the numerous commercial colossi in resorts, such as the Wisconsin Dells, there are also several civic colossi in the state. I am grateful to George Ewing, Jr., for calling the splendid loon in Mercer, Wisconsin, to my attention.

Dick Johnson, quoted by Jim Klobuchar, *Minneapolis Star and Tribune*, April 26, 1983, p. 1B. **99**

Minneapolis Star and Tribune, April 26, 1983, p. 1B. **100**

Larry Batson, " 'Eagle Capital of the World' throws a monumental wing-ding," *Minneapolis Tribune*, July 17, 1983, p. 1B. For civic boosterism, see Yi-Fu Tuan, *Topophilia, A Study of Environmental Perception, Attitudes, and Values* (Englewood Cliffs, New Jersey: Prentice-Hall, Inc., 1974), pp. 201-4. **101**

Minneapolis Tribune, July 17, 1983, p. 1B. **102**

103   Gary Wigdahl, *Twixt Hill and Prairie: A Century of Challenge in the Rothsay, Minnesota Area* (Rothsay, Minnesota: Holiday Printing, 1982), pp. 283-86. I am grateful to Marilyn McGriff, of the Isanti County Historical Society, for calling this book and other local histories to my attention.

104   "Today's Hero in Rothsay, Minn.," *Minneapolis Tribune*, April 24, 1976, p. 1A.

105   "Ugh! For the Jolly Green Statue," an editorial from the *Mankato Free Press*, in *Minneapolis Star*, April 14, 1978, p. 8A.

106   "Out and Away," *Minneapolis Tribune*, September 1, 1974, p. 1F.

107   "Minnesota Festivals '83," *Minneapolis Tribune*, May 29, 1983, p. 6E.

108   "11th Annual Cambridge Swedish Festival," *The Scotsman*, May 30, 1983.

109   Marilyn and Ron McGriff were kind enough to answer my questions about the Cambridge festival, and kept me informed about various goings-on there in the summer of 1983. They are not responsible for my interpretation of the data, however, although I hope to persuade them that Cambridge needs a colossus.

110   Information on the loon is taken from the text of a postcard published by McKenna of Virginia, Virginia, Minnesota. Bill Martin of Virginia designed this unique colossus. It is made of fiberglass applied over a metal framework. Larry Gentelli assisted in the construction. The blue and white banners on the streets leading to Olcott Park were in place when I visited Virginia in June 1983.

111   Jim Kimball, "Crane Lake's Voyageur Day is Memorable Experience," *Minneapolis Morning Tribune*, July 17, 1964, p. 13.

112   "Olivia: Newton-John, that is, will attend 'Corn Capital Days'," *Minneapolis Tribune*, June 8, 1978, p. 2B and "Worth Noting," *Minneapolis Star*, July 24, 1978, p. 6B.

113   See notices of "Cornland, USA" and "Plowville '75" in Olivia in *Minneapolis Tribune*, August 24, 1975, p. 10F and *Minneapolis Tribune*, September 8, 1974, p. 10F.

114   The site adjoins the cemetery and the hill from which the Olivia water tower rises. The acreage is itself a kind of no-man's-land in terms of both agriculture and potential commercial use—a zone of transition from the cornfields to the settlement. That frontier zone is occupied by the truly leisured—picnickers and the dearly departed. The citizens of Olivia occupy the active terrain on either side of the colossus.

115   Wigdahl, *Twixt Hill and Prairie* (1982), p. 284.

116   The colossi in Crosby, Madison, Kelliher, Vergas, Baudette, Thief River Falls, Garrison, Akeley, International Falls, Virginia, Mora, Fergus Falls, Pelican Rapids, and Erskine stand in long-established city parks or fairgrounds along the highway, and picnic places are provided as a matter of course. The statues at Battle Lake, Cloquet, Hackensack, and several other locations occupy the grounds of tourist information offices operated by the Chamber of Commerce or other civic groups. Special picnic parks have been newly created around the statues in Blue Earth, Ortonville, Deerwood, Nevis, Menahga, Ray, Olivia, and Wheaton.

A fiberglass Paul Bunyan look-alike in Littlefork, Minnesota. Photo by Liz Harrison.

Nick Coleman, "State's statues: a bit fishy, but mostly unforgettable," *Minneapolis Tribune*, August 22, 1982, p. 1B.

Mr. Bruns was the prime mover behind the Long Lake Loon (Vergas) and the otter in his hometown, Fergus Falls. I am grateful to Mr. Bruns for his encouragement and for his tips on finding Minnesota colossi.

"Big Vic statue installed as land protest," *Minneapolis Tribune*, May 14, 1980, p. 2B, an Associated Press story with a photograph of the statue wafting through the air beneath a Bell 205 helicopter.

"Duluth: Canadian fined for flying statue to Voyageurs National Park," *Minneapolis Tribune*, December 11, 1980, p. 3B and "Canadian pilot's fine for moving statue is reduced," *Minneapolis Tribune*, March 5, 1981, p. 3B.

"International Falls: U.S. officials upset over Voyageurs statue," *Minneapolis Tribune*, May 19, 1982, pp. 3-4C.

"Duluth: Jury rules U.S. should pay man who has defied park service," *Minneapolis Tribune*, May 29, 1982, p. 3C.

"N.D. entrepreneur hopes to attract those who want to ogle Og," *Minneapolis Star and Tribune*, December 20, 1982, p. 2B.

The management of the Plains Motel has kindly responded by telephone to my inquiries about the fiberglass pheasant that adorns the premises. It was made for a prior owner by an itinerant sculptor, possibly a Native American, around 1958. It has been repainted several times, and a new postcard is currently being prepared. "Albert," who stands beside Route 71, is mentioned in Stern, *Amazing America* (1978), p. 263. Sue Beckham, of River Falls, Wisconsin, took charge of investigations at Hayward and turned up the quoted postcard text, which describes the dimensions of the fish with such relish that no space remains for the standard "wish you were here" message. It was published by G. R. Brown Co., Eau Claire, Wisconsin. My old friend, Professor Warren I. Susman, of Rutgers University, tells me that his favorite colossus is "The Largest Manure Pile in the World," in Sioux City, Iowa. He claims to cherish a postcard view thereof.

117

118

119

120

121

122

123

124   A weekly television program based on the old Robert R. Ripley syndicated cartoon featured the Darwin twine ball and the competing ball in Cawker City, Kansas, during the 1982-83 season on the ABC Network. The colossal cow in Harvard, Illinois, figured as a milestone in the coverage of a cross-country bicycle race featured on ABC's *Wide World of Sports* in February 1984.

     Despite its titular claims, one of the mass of signs displayed with the 17-ton cheddar says that the cheese was eaten in 1965 at a convention. Whether that implies nibbling or total consumption (!) is a moot point. The object in the trailer *could* be a cheese. For the other elements of the Neillsville ensemble, see note 98, above.

125   Paul Fussell, *Abroad, British Literary Traveling Between the Wars* (New York: Oxford University Press, 1980), p. 167, cites Roger Welsch's *Tall-Tale Postcards* (1976) for the early dating. Hal Morgan, *Big Time: American Tall-Tale Postcards* (New York: St. Martin's Press, Inc., 1981), unpaginated, suggests that production stayed high and was concentrated in the Midwest. Cynthia Elyce Rubin, "The Midwestern Corn Palaces: A 'Maize' of Detail and Wonder," *The Clarion* (Fall, 1983), pp. 24-25, illustrates two turn-of-the-century postcards produced in Kansas and Iowa. The former depicts an ear of corn as large as a farm wagon; the latter, ears so large they must be sawed into kernels by a two-man team.

126   Valerie Monahan, *An American Postcard Collector's Guide* (Poole, Dorset: Blandford Press, 1981), plate 3, in an unpaginated plate section following p. 48, shows a "Carload of Strawberries" card (nine berries fill an "S.P." flatcar, and the writer is given a blank line on which to indicate where this extraordinary sight was seen) published in 1909 by Edward H. Mitchell, San Francisco. My North Dakota postcard (ca. 1920) is the prototype for a 1950s card, also in my collection, showing the same potato (minus the sign) on a B. & A. flatcar, and titled "Aroostook Potato—The Kind We Grow in Maine."

127   The Iowa card ("You can hardly believe it!") is published by the Dunlap Post Card Co., Omaha, Nebraska, as is the Kansas image ("Wheatland, U.S.A."). Minnesota fish cards are produced by NMN, Inc. of Crosslake, Minnesota, and are overprinted with the name of the specific town in which the card is sold. Occasionally, one finds racks of such cards that have not been overprinted, leaving the sender free to designate the locus of the fish story. The Ben Franklin store in Olivia, Minnesota, yielded several kinds of tall-tale fish and pheasant cards with blank vignettes for do-it-yourself captions.

128   The postcard is published by the W. A. Fisher Co., Virginia, Minnesota.

129   Fussell, *Abroad* (1980), p. 167.

130   Stern, *Amazing America* (1978), p. 445.

131   See Ernestine G. Miller, ed., *The Art of Advertising, Great Commercial Illustrations From the Early Years of Magazines* (New York: St. Martin's Press, 1980), unpaginated ads from the *Ladies' Home Journal* for Royal Baking Powder (May, 1923), Kirk's Flake White Soap (May, 1919), and Adams' California Fruit Gum (September, 1920).

132   *This Fabulous Century, 1920-1930*, Vol. 3 (New York: Time-Life Books, 1969), p. 269.

133   Harden Bryant Leachman, *The Early Advertising Scene* (Wood Dale, Illinois: The Story Book Press, 1949), p. 100.

Hannah Campbell, *"Why Did They Name It . . . ?"* (New York: Ace Books, 1964), p. 161.   134

Frank Rowsome, Jr., *The Verse by the Side of the Road, The Story of the Burma-Shave Signs and Jingles* (Brattleboro, Vermont: Stephen Greene Press, 1965), pp. 19 and 72.   135

I am grateful to the Hustead family, current owners of Wall Drug, for answering my many questions. The signs are today far less numerous than they were in the past, although they still turn up in some strange places. A photograph in the Wall Drug files taken in 1981 shows a sign along one of the canals in Amsterdam, Holland, and the legend: "5,397 miles to Wall Drug, Wall, South Dakota, U.S.A." It is by no means unique!   136

Hugh E. Agnew, *Outdoor Advertising* (New York: McGraw-Hill Book Company, Inc., 1938), pp. 123, 144-45, and 272.   137

John Margolies, *The End of the Road, Vanishing Highway Architecture in America*, exhibition catalog (New York: Penguin Books/The Hudson River Museum, 1981), p. 21.   138

This is the argument advanced by David Gebhard in his excellent introduction to Jim Heimann and Rip Georges, *California Crazy, Roadside Vernacular Architecture* (San Francisco: Chronicle Books, 1980), p. 19.   139

Warren James Belasco, *Americans on the Road, From Autocamp to Motel, 1910-1945* (Cambridge, Massachusetts: MIT Press, 1981), p. 159. See also J. J. C. Andrews, *The Well-Built Elephant and Other Roadside Attractions, a Tribute to American Eccentricity* (New York: Congdon & Weed, 1984), esp. pp. 14-19, 42-43, 68-72, 90-91, and 96-101.   140

Margolies, *The End of the Road* (1981), plates 117-125, esp. plates 121 and 124; and Heimann and Georges, *California Crazy* (1980), pp. 108 and 117.   141

Daniel L. Vieyra, *"Fill 'er Up": An Architectural History of America's Gas Stations* (New York: Collier Books, 1979), unpaginated plate section following p. 50, plausibly dates the surviving shell-shaped gas station in Winston-Salem, North Carolina, to the 1930s. Shell Oil did use a slightly larger version for its corporate building at the California Exposition, Balboa Park, San Diego, in 1935; see illustration in Heimann and Georges, *California Crazy* (1980), p. 80.   142

See note 7, above.   143

O. E. Rolvaag, *Giants in the Earth, A Saga of the Prairie* (New York: Harper and Row/Perennial Classics, 1965), p. 6. The novel (1924-1925) was translated from the Norwegian and first published in the United States in 1927.   144

For discussion and illustration of the various roadside ice palaces, see Gebhard, introduction to Heimann and Georges (1980), pp. 19, 20, and 24; Heimann and Georges, *California Crazy* (1980), pp. 46-47; and Margolies, *End of the Road* (1981), plate 74.   145

F. Scott Fitzgerald, "The Ice Palace," in *Flappers and Philosophers* (New York: Charles Scribner's Sons, 1959), pp. 57 and 66. The collection was originally published in 1920 and the story first appeared in the *Saturday Evening Post* in May, 1920.   146

Kate Johnson, "Fire and Ice," *Architecture Minnesota*, 9, #1 (January/February,   147

1983), p. 35. See also the first views of the ice palaces with fireworks and other early stereopticon images in Sara Rath, *Pioneer Photographer, Wisconsin's H. H. Bennett* (Wisconsin Dells: H. H. Bennett Studio, 1979), pp. 57, 134, and 135. Many illustrations are found in Fred Anderes and Ann Agranoff, *Ice Palaces* (New York: Abbeville Press, 1983). Rubin, "Midwestern Corn Palaces" (1983), pp. 26-27, provides illustrations that suggest a close correlation between ice and corn palaces in both date and style. This information provides some independent support for my associations of scale, frontier, and the Midwest.

148   Fitzgerald, "The Ice Palace" (1920), p. 54 and 66.

149   The lemons (and oranges), the pig, the dog, the Sphinx, "Mammy," and related examples are frequently illustrated. See, for example, Heimann and Georges, *California Crazy* (1980), pp. 62, 81, 114, 115, and 96; Margolies, *End of the Road* (1981), plates 54, 55, and 61; and Vieyra, *"Fill 'er Up"* (1979), unpaginated plate following p. 50.

150   Margolies, *End of the Road* (1981), p. 18. Mammy's Cupboard, on old Highway 61, is called "Black Mammy" by those who live nearby. Gebhard, introduction to Heimann and Georges (1980), reproduces, among a great number of patented buildings of this type, a skirted Mexican dancer (Patent No. 86683) by Sadie O'Neil of Seattle, Washington (1931). The U.S. Patent Office also has a category of applications called "Buildings simulating vehicles" that contains a 1931 dirigible-building by Nickolas Lagios (No. 86617) and an airplane-gas station of 1930 by J. Smith (No. 84304). Professor Joe Corn, Program in Values, Technology and Society, Stanford University, kindly shared his research into these futuristic vehicular structures with me.

151   J. Edward Tufft, "The Mother Goose Pantry," *Wayside Salesman*, 1 (November, 1931), p. 20.

152   West, *Day of the Locust* (1939), p. 93.

153   "The Great American Roadside," *Fortune* (1934), pp. 61 and 172.

154   For an insightful introduction to Venturi's theories and to the semiotic dimensions of architecture, see Charles Jencks, *The Language of Post-Modern Architecture* (New York: Rizzoli, 1977), esp. "The Modes of Architectural Communication," pp. 39-85, and plate 65.

155   For the artifactual response of the popular imagination to the discovery of Tut's tomb in 1922, see Bevis Hillier, *The World of Art Deco*, exhibition catalog (New York: E. P. Dutton, 1971), p. 33 ff.

156   For a trenchant analysis of the film and of Robert Armstrong's famous tag line (" 'Twas beauty killed the beast."), see Roger Dooley, *From Scarface to Scarlett, American Films in the 1930s* (New York: Harcourt Brace Jovanovich, 1981), p. 380.

157   West, *Day of the Locust* (1939), pp. 138-39 and 79-80. See also "Great Sphinx Hole, Wacky Golf, Panama City Beach, Florida" [undated], and other photographs by John Margolies, in *Synthetic Links*, an exhibition of color photographs that opened at the Institute for Urban Resources, Inc., Long Island City, in September, 1983.

158   West, *Day of the Locust* (1939), p. 81. See Jim Heimann, *Hooray! for Hollywood, A Postcard Tour of Hollywood's Golden Era* (San Francisco: Chronicle Books, 1983), p. 50, for a view of the backlot at Fox Studios, made in the 30s.

The historiography of "kitsch" is established in Gillo Dorfles, *Kitsch, The World of Bad Taste* (New York: Universe Books, 1969), p. 7. Dorfles reprints Broch's "Notes on the Problem of Kitsch," pp. 49-76, and Greenberg's "The Avant-Garde and Kitsch," pp. 116-26. I am grateful to Colleen Sheehy, a graduate student in the Program in American Studies, the University of Minnesota, for sharing with me her interesting unpublished paper, " 'Kitsch' Reconsidered: Pink Flamingos, Plastic Chickens and Other Lawn Ornaments."   159

Jacques Sternberg, *Kitsch* (New York: St. Martin's Press, 1972), unpaginated introduction.   160

Harold Rosenberg, "Pop Culture: Kitsch Criticism," in *The Tradition of the New* (New York: McGraw-Hill, 1965), pp. 264-66. The essay was written in 1960.   161

Old photographs showing Liberty's torch-wielding arm, exhibited in splendid isolation at the Philadelphia Centennial Exposition of 1876 in aid of a fund-raising campaign to finance construction of her pedestal could, perhaps, be mistaken for promotional views of a roadhouse, somewhere west of the Hudson River, touting flame-broiled steaks. Modern taste is inured to worse excesses! Trachtenberg, *The Statue of Liberty* (1976), plate 70, reprints an extraordinary photograph of the arm, as do many students of kitsch. Other equally evocative contemporary photographs of the Statue of Liberty in pieces or being assembled appear in Julia Van Haaften, "The Making of *Liberty*," *Portfolio*, 3, #4 (July/August, 1981), pp. 46-49.   162

Little of substance has been written on Borglum and the Mt. Rushmore project. For a summary of the literature, see Libby W. Seaburg, "Artists' Biographies and Bibliographies," in *200 Years of American Sculpture* (1976), pp. 260-61. Of some additional interest is Lincoln Borglum, *My Father's Mountain, Mt. Rushmore National Memorial and How It Was Carved* (n.l.: privately printed, 1966), unpaginated. The interpretation of Mt. Rushmore offered here is my own. For the Statue of Liberty, see Trachtenberg, *The Statue of Liberty* (1976), and note 64, above.

From an article by Borglum in *World's Work*, quoted by McSpadden, *Famous Sculptors of America* (1924), p. 232.   163

Gutzon Borglum, "Moulding a Mountain," *Forum*, 70, #4 (October, 1923), p. 2019.   164

Editorial comment appended to Borglum, "Moulding a Mountain," *Forum* (1923), p. 2020.   165

Borglum, "Moulding a Mountain," *Forum* (1923), p. 2025.   166

"Sculpturing a Mountain," *The Nation*, 105, #2719 (August 9, 1917), p. 140.   167

"Uncivil War Over the Confederate Memorial," *Literary Digest*, 84, #11 (March 14, 1925), pp. 28-30.   168

"Uncivil War," *Literary Digest* (1925), p. 30.   169

Lincoln Borglum, *My Father's Mountain* (1966), unpaginated.   170

Gutzon Borglum, "Mountain Sculpture," *Scientific American*, 148, #1 (January, 1933), p. 7.   171

[The Drifter], "In the Driftway," *The Nation*, 135, #3520 (December 21, 1932), p. 618.   172

173   The Crazy Horse Memorial, outside Custer, South Dakota, is a related landmark. Carved by Korczak Ziolkowski, who expected to finish the work in 1978 (he did not), the figure in the round literally replaced Thunderhead Mountain. Chief Crazy Horse,who defeated Custer at Little Big Horn in 1876, is depicted mounted on a galloping buffalo pony. The colossal pictures annually drawn in local grains and grasses on the exterior of the Corn Palace in Mitchell, South Dakota, reflect this same aesthetic sensibility. Since two local businessmen conceived of the idea in 1892, the entire building, used as the municipal auditorium, has been covered in a fresh sheath of corn each year to celebrate the harvest. The 11 pictorial panels are specially decorated for the Corn Palace Festival, held during the last week in September. See *Reader's Digest Illustrated Guide to the Treasures of America* (Pleasantville, New York: The Reader's Digest Association, Inc., 1974), pp. 360 and 369.

174   David Gebhard and Tom Martinson, *A Guide to the Architecture of Minnesota* (Minneapolis, Minnesota: University of Minnesota Press, 1977), pp. 31-32.

175   Commissioned in 1932, the monument was dedicated in 1936. The size of the statue was its chief marketable feature in the 1950s, when the Tourist Bureau of the St. Paul Chamber of Commerce used "Onyx John" as its promotional emblem. See Garvey, "From *God of Peace* to *Onyx John*," (1978), pp. 15-17.

176   Trachtenberg, *The Statue of Liberty* (1976), esp. pp. 108 and 112-14. For popular postcards (ca. 1940), delighting in and confirming this ambiguity of siting, see Kerry Tucker, *Greetings from New York, A Visit to Manhattan in Postcards* (New York: Delilah Books/G. P. Putnam's Sons, 1981), pp. 14-15.

177   Curtis F. Brown, *Star-Spangled Kitsch* (New York: Universe Books, 1975), p. 100. Brown also illustrates the Los Angeles Sphinx (p. 104) and a liquor bottle shaped like Mt. Rushmore (p. 186). On the latter, he comments: "As though Mount Rushmore weren't kitschy enough, a distiller has turned that monster monument into an iridescent bourbon bottle." On Lafferty's elephants, see also Julian Cavalier, "Elephants Remembered," *Historic Preservation,* 29 (January/March, 1977), pp. 39-43.

178   The Coney Island elephant is illustrated and discussed in Brown, *Star-Spangled Kitsch* (1975), p. 100. It is also discussed in Andrews, *The Well-Built Elephant* (1984), pp. 14-19.

        See also, in regard to circus animals and Lucy-buildings, Charles E. Funnell, *By the Beautiful Sea, the Rise and High Times of That Great American Resort, Atlantic City* (New Brunswick, N.J.: Rutgers University Press, 1983), p. 58.

179   Rem Koolhaas, *Delirious New York, A Retroactive Manifesto for Manhattan* (New York: Oxford University Press, 1978), p. 28. Charles Jencks, *Bizarre Architecture* (New York: Rizzoli International Publications, Inc., 1979), pp.61-64, calls product-shaped buildings "delirious trademarks."

180   John F. Kasson, *Amusing the Million, Coney Island at the Turn of the Century* (New York: Hill & Wang, 1978), p. 33.

181   William Ouelette, *Fantasy Postcards* (Garden City, New York: Doubleday & Co., Inc., 1975), plate 25 and notes. A miniaturized Heinz pickle lapel pin was the most popular souvenir of the 1939 New York World's Fair.

        Vignette postcards originated in Germany and were often printed there for American firms. View cards made at the turn of the century, whether domestic or foreign in origin, frequently relied on the vignette technique. A 1911 card issued by Edward Mitchell of San Francisco shows the city of Portland, Oregon, nestled in the heart of a giant rose. Another contemporary example of the technique depicts the major buildings of Baltimore inscribed on a massive four-leaf clover. See Dorothy B. Ryan, *Picture Postcards in the United States, 1893-1918* (New York: Clarkson N. Potter, Inc., 1982), pp. 154, 163, and unpaginated plate section following p. 216. These are not unrelated to the "jackalope," the big fish, and various other tall-tale postcards of the Midwest.

For an investigation of the linen-finish tourist postcards of the 1920s and 30s insofar as they relate to fantastic roadside buildings, and the report of an interview with the creator-proprietor of Mammy Gas, see John Baeder, *Gas, Food, and Lodging* (New York: Abbeville Press, 1982), esp. pp. 19, 58-59, 72-76, 82-83, and 92-93.   182

Baeder's *Diners* (New York: Harry N. Abrams, Inc., 1978) discusses and reproduces the author's own paintings of roadside diners. It was during the course of preparing this book that Baeder began to collect, to study, and finally to imitate the appearance of linen-finish postcards in his work. See pp. 96-112 for an account of his growing fascination with the surreal settings and electric colors of roadside greetings.

Warren H. Anderson, *Vanishing Roadside America* (Tucson, Arizona: University of Arizona Press, 1981), is a collection of the author's colored drawings imitating the style of linen-finish cards but depicting, for the most part, old neon signs shown in tight closeup. One of the most evocative of the lot is "The Indians Seldom Smile," pp. 102-3, a drawing of a one-of-a-kind sign depicting Fraser's *End of the Trail*. This neon sign was mounted above the Trail's End Motel in Big Spring, Texas:

> But now a frontier of a different sort has made its mark. The Interstate
> has bypassed the old highway and this motel has met the end of its trail.
> The sign most aptly symbolizes the status of the place. Just down the road
> a motel sign containing a typical smiling cowboy has already vanished.
> His neon adversary barely survives.

Koolhaas, *Delirious New York* (1978), p. 28.   183

See Kasson, *Amusing the Million* (1978), p. 83. For the imitation and reuse of the sculptural facade of Coney Island's "Dreamland," see the "Dreamland" at the 1901 Buffalo Pan-American Exposition, in John Allwood, *The Great Exhibitions* (London: Studio Vista, 1977), p. 106. There is a sense in which Simon Rodia's Watts Towers of ca. 1920-1948 are fantasy colossi in the amusement park tradition, infused with a drive to become national landmarks. Rodia's oblique explanation of his monument suggests as much: "I had in mind to do something big, and I did. I wanted to do something for the United States. . . . " See Michael Webb, "Saving Simon Rodia's Towers," *Portfolio*, 5, #4 (July/August, 1983), pp.68-71.   184

The Greatest of Expositions (1904), pp. 192, 200, and 204.   185

Benedict, Dobkin, and Armstrong, *A Catalogue of Posters* (1982), entries F2, 5, 8 and 10.   186

For the colossi of the 1939 New York World's Fair, see Helen A. Harrison, *Dawn of a New Day, The New York World's Fair, 1939/40*, exhibition catalog (New York: New York University Press/The Queens Museum, 1980), pp. 112 and 114. The largest of the Fair colossi at Flushing was a 65-foot tall white statue of George Washington. A small-scale model by academic sculptor James Earle   187

James Earle Fraser's colossal *George Washington* at the 1939 New York World's Fair. From an amateur snapshot in the collection of the author.

Fraser was blown up to huge scale to serve as a centerpiece for Constitution Mall, the main fairgrounds thoroughfare. For Fraser's statue and overblown Washington lore of the 1920s and 30s in general, see Karal Ann Marling, "Of Cherry Trees and Ladies' Teas: Grant Wood Looks at Colonial America," forthcoming in Alan Axelrod, ed., *The Colonial Revival in America* (Winterthur, Delaware: Winterthur Museum/W. W. Norton & Co., 1984).

For Cobb's Chicken House, see Heimann and Georges, *California Crazy* (1980), p. 80. For the pageantry and architecture of the Disney parks, see Valerie Childs, *The Magic of Disneyland and Disneyworld* (New York: Mayflower Books, n.d.), unpaginated plates; Christopher Finch, *Walt Disney's America* (New York: Abbeville Press, Inc., 1978), esp. pp. 45 and 51-64; and Michael Albert's discussion of Florida theme parks, including Disneyworld, as covert statements or as dramas in which "the dominance of man over nature" is played out, in "The Transformation of the Roadside Attraction" (1981).

188   The hobo song, closely related to the railroad ballad popular during the enforced mobility of the 1930s, is discussed in Norm Cohen, *Long Steel Rail, The Railroad in American Folksong* (Urbana: University of Illinois Press, 1981), p. 343. Harry McClintock, sometimes credited with writing "Big Rock Candy Mountain," recorded hobo songs in the late 1920s and early 30s.

189   This consideration of the roadside colossus as a temporal, spatial, and imaginative frontier amplifies my earlier discussions of literary and artifactual manifestations of frontier interest in the 1920s and 30s. See Karal Ann Marling, "*My Egypt*, The Irony of the American Dream," *Winterthur Portfolio*, 15, 1 (Spring, 1980), pp. 25-39, which, leaning heavily on *The Great Gatsby*, explores a painterly frontier, where personal biography and national history touch; and "Thomas Hart Benton's *Boomtown*: Regionalism Redefined," *Prospects, An Annual of American Cultural Studies*, 6, Jack Salzman, ed. (New York: Burt Franklin & Co., Inc., 1981), pp. 73-137, which treats of frontier place as permeable time in the popular cultural and cinematic milieu of Regionalist art.

Karal Ann Marling received her Ph.D. in art history at Bryn Mawr College in 1971. She has taught at Case Western Reserve University and Vassar College, and is now professor of art history and American studies at the University of Minnesota. Marling is the author of *Wall-to-Wall America: A Cultural History of Post-Office Murals in the Great Depression* (Minnesota, 1982).

THE
COLOSSUS
OF ROADS

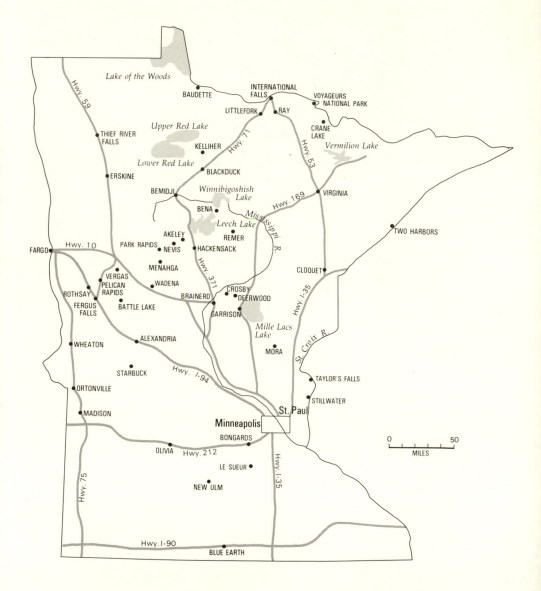

MINNESOTA COLOSSI

(Bold-face p. nos. indicate illustrations.)

OTHER COLOSSI

The Big Fish Supper Club near Bena, Minnesota, was homemade, in tarpaper.

At the falls of the Pelican River in downtown Pelican Rapids stands the resident pelican.

Erskine's concrete fish is beached in a lakefront park.

This fantastic creature appears to have slithered out of Serpent Lake, in Crosby, Minnesota.

This giant strawberry ice-cream cone stands beside the road near Wadena.

Since 1954, Hackensack has been the home of LucetteDiana Kensack, "Paul Bunyan's Sweetheart."

Brainerd's talking Paul Bunyan sits in a rustic log temple, adorned with a fresco depicting Babe, his pet ox. The ensemble is, of course, a burlesque version of the Lincoln Memorial.

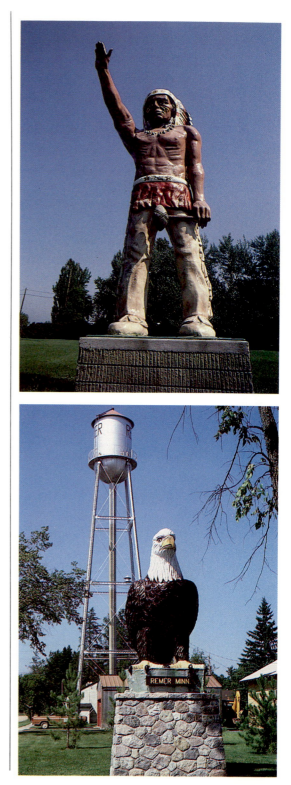

Chief Wenonga, in fiberglass, stops tourists on the road to Battle Lake.

Among Minnesota's newest colossi, the Remer eagle was dedicated in the summer of 1983. It is one of many products of Creative Display, Inc., of Sparta, Wisconsin.

This giant ear of corn put Olivia on the tourist map of the Midwest.

The Long Lake Loon was a community project sponsored by the Vergas Fire Department. The statue was dedicated in 1963 to the memory of a former town postmaster.

20-foot Pierre, the Talking Voyageur of Two Harbors, dates from 1959.

The Rothsay prairie chicken, in brilliant display, was designed and fabricated locally as a 1976 Bicentennial project.

The Crane Lake Commercial Club decided to erect a monument to the Voyageur in 1958. The statue was made to order in fiberglass by Sculptured Advertising, Inc., of Minneapolis.

Wheaton's 26-foot-tall concrete mallard was built in 1959 at a cost of $1,200. It was designed by Bob Bruns of Fergus Falls, a connoisseur of Midwestern colossi, working from "a paperweight, a Grain Belt Beer ad, and a dime-store statue."

The Jolly Green Giant was set up along Interstate-90 in Blue Earth, Minnesota, in 1978.

This statue honors the spanking new legend of St. Urho (said to have driven the grasshoppers out of Finland!) and was carved in laminated oak by chainsaw artist Jerry Ward in 1982. "He's just as authentic as the Jolly Green Giant . . . or Bemidji's Paul Bunyan," quipped the editor of the Menahga newspaper.

This 3,000-pound reminder of Mora's Swedish heritage was built by the Jaycees in 1971 "as a tourist attraction": the commemorative plaque affixed to the statue says so.

Big Ole, Alexandria's 28-foot mascot, promotes belief in the authenticity of the Kensington Runestone, evidence for the "discovery" of America in the 14th century by the Vikings. Ole used to wear a Santa suit at Christmas time.